Again in a Heartbeat

Again in a Heartbeat

a memoir of love, loss and dating again

Susan G. Weidener

Acknowledgments

I began this book in the summer of 2007 when I participated in a writing retreat sponsored by Women Writing for (a) Change. Spending six days in the Kentucky countryside with my laptop and other women writers was exactly what I needed after sixteen years as a reporter. I had left *The Philadelphia Inquirer* and wanted to explore a more creative form of writing than journalism.

I knew I wanted to write about my husband, John Cavalieri, losing him to cancer after a seven-year ordeal and then trying to find my way as a single mother and middle-aged woman on my own. It was there in the serenity of the writing retreat that I began to understand the power of memoir and how it transforms and helps make sense of our lives. The answers were always within me; I just needed to put down in words the experiences that shaped me . . . especially the dream of meeting Prince Charming . . . and then what to do when he makes a dramatic and tragic exit.

Susan G. Weidener

Countless thanks go to the many women who read this book and offered support and guidance, especially Mary Pierce Brosmer, author and founder of Women Writing for (a) Change; Lorraine Margaret Owczarzak, who edited the first draft, and Kate Raley, who edited a later version. They offered invaluable insight into the craft and art of storytelling so different from my cut-and-dried world of journalistic reporting.

I also owe thanks to my friend Susan Bragner who designed the cover illustration of forsythia; Cynthia McGroarty, a former *Inquirer* colleague who writes fiction and nonfiction and teaches creative writing; and Johanna Smith, a family therapist, who offered guidance on how better to write about loss and grieving.

Above all, gratitude goes to John, who wrote about honor and courage and his battle with cancer in the years before his death at the age of forty-seven. His words leap off these pages. He was and still is my touchstone to truth, chivalry and love.

Finally, to my two wonderful sons, Alex and Daniel, thank you for your love and support. Without it, I never could have written this book.

A Note From The Author

The lives and conversations depicted here have been reconstructed from memory. I have changed several of the names and identifying characteristics of the people in this book. These are my memories and may differ from others' memories of those same conversations.

Prologue

If my life were a movie, how would I change it? The answer is I wouldn't. Unless, I could have saved John.

Before John, I had little experience with men. It was John who taught me about myself. You aren't as strong and confident as you want people to believe, he said.

It was John who gave me everything a woman could want in a man. A bouquet of yellow roses with a hand-printed card. "Happy Wednesday."

John came to me when I least expected it. John left me when I least expected it. Not that it was his fault. But I blamed him anyway. Ghosts of regret haunt my memories. That day in the kitchen, me shouting, "I wish I'd never met you!"

Perhaps, I have been too hard on myself. John said I was. But being hard on myself is part of the woman I am. "I should have done more," I told my friends. "I could have been kinder."

To escape from my grief, I tried to fill the empty space left by John. Much of the time, I wasn't escaping anything – just changing places, changing skirts, changing months, changing nothing.

The first time I saw John he was standing under white dogwood trees at Valley Forge Military Academy. He held himself very tall with a presence.

Arrested by his ease and confidence, I felt a jolt as John's dark eyes locked onto mine. I wanted to look away but he wouldn't let me. Who was this man? From this, arises my story.

PART ONE

Chapter One

"**H**ow have you been?" John asked.

I was not surprised to hear his voice on the other end of the phone. It had been a week since we met at Valley Forge Military Academy.

"Busy. My editor has been sending me out to community events and school board meetings."

"Do you like working for a newspaper?" he asked.

"It's my first job as a reporter. I feel almost like it's a calling. Or at least that's one way to rationalize my whopping $140 week salary," I joked.

The year was 1977. Although I dreamed of becoming a famous novelist, I had fallen in love with Woodward and Bernstein after watching the Watergate hearings. Local journalism seemed a way to write *and* get published. Now I was a staff writer for the *Suburban and Wayne Times*, a family-run newspaper located in Wayne, Pennsylvania, the town on Philadelphia's Main Line where I grew up.

The monotony of school board and township meetings had been offset by interviews with Chubby Checker, who lived in the area, and Bob Hope, who visited Valley Forge Military Academy. I also covered the filming of *Taps*, a movie shot at the academy, starring two unknowns, Sean Penn and Tom Cruise.

John laughed. "You're a good writer. I read your stuff all the time. Hey, I was calling to ask you to go dancing."

"Excuse me?"

Although I was flattered by John's interest in me, I was seeing Alan, my editor, who was old enough to be my father.

"I'm not big on dancing," I told him. "Too many formal dances Dad made me go to at Valley Forge."

"How about dinner?"

I paused, considered. "That would be fine."

He showed up wearing a black blazer with the West Point insignia over the breast pocket and creased gray slacks. He resembled the actor Jeff Goldblum. He had a mustache and wore dark green aviator sunglasses.

Over dinner at an Italian restaurant with fresh red and white carnations on the table, John told me he was chairman of the English Department.

"My father had that same job at Valley Forge before he became dean there."

"I've heard about your dad," John said. "Didn't he teach English to J.D. Salinger?"

"Yes. And Edward Albee."

John nodded. "Your father was an institution at the academy. A real academician is how everyone describes him."

"He majored in Latin and English and was Phi Beta Kappa from the University of Pennsylvania. Can you believe it? My dad, the liberal intellectual, ends up at a military academy."

John was a good listener. He never took his eyes off me.

"You're beautiful," he said. "Did anyone ever tell you that your eyes are almost green?"

I was embarrassed. My mother always told me that beautiful women had upturned noses and long, flowing hair like the girls in the Breck commercials. I had neither. I knew my looks were attractive, but not classically beautiful.

College had been a series of infatuations. I was easy prey for men with bedroom eyes and a taste for good books and music. I liked the men more than they liked me.

"Thank you for dinner. The food was good, don't you think?"

"Oh, I see. You don't want to answer my question about your eyes."

I fidgeted, folded the linen napkin in my lap and placed it on the table. Why were his eyes boring into mine? What did he want?

John smiled. "Yes, the pasta was good."

By the time the check arrived, we had been talking for close to two hours.

"Why aren't you in the Army?" I asked.

"Two weeks before I graduated from West Point, they informed me I wouldn't be commissioned," he said.

He looked away. "I was diagnosed with ulcerative colitis the spring of my senior year. I wanted to be an Airborne Ranger, career soldier. I could have done a desk job, but they wouldn't even let me do that. They told me I should be grateful. I had gotten a free education at the taxpayers' expense. I didn't want or need their goddamn free education."

He quickly picked up the check and pulled out his credit card to pay for dinner.

"That was six years ago," he said.

He could see my concern. "I have one of the best doctors in Philadelphia. The colitis is under control although I have an occasional flare-up."

I had heard the word 'colitis' before but had no idea what ulcerative colitis was. We got up to leave. It was a warm summer night. I could smell his aftershave, a sweet, sexy smell like apricots. Billowy clouds were framed by pink light as the sun began to set. His fingers briefly touched my wrist. "I want to see you again," he said.

Chapter Two

John and I both had a week of vacation. It was July, the humid Pennsylvania air sapping me of energy. I think the idea to head to Canada was mine, an impulsive "let's do it," kind of thing. I had never been to Canada before. Neither had John.

We drove through New York in John's dark green British MGB sports car with the tan canvas top. John drove expertly, if not a bit too fast.

When we got to Montreal, we had vodka and tonics and burgers at an outdoor café. People were speaking French and strolling down tree-lined sidewalks in sandals and jeans. I took in a deep breath of cool Canadian air.

"Why did my compliment about your eyes when we were having dinner bother you?" John asked.

I looked away. "It didn't," I lied.

He smiled. "So tell me more about yourself. What was it like growing up at the academy?"

"My father set me up with one blind date after another at dances," I laughed. "I had to wear evening gowns in red velvet and aqua taffeta while everyone else was in jeans and tie-dyes. I even had long white gloves that came up to my elbows. When I got home, I tore off my gown and dreamed that Paul McCartney was in love with me."

He leaned back after I was finished. "I'll bet you were gorgeous in those evening gowns."

I kept smiling as he gazed at me. Why tell him the truth? I was taller than most of the boys. Dad insisted I go to those dances. He brought home a manila folder filled with cadets' pictures and their grade point averages so I could select my date.

Usually, my blind date and I made the best of an awkward situation, doing the box step and making dumb jokes about military schools. While everyone else was dancing to "I Want to Hold Your Hand," our fate was "Moon River" sung by a middle-aged woman in a cavernous ballroom reeking of floor wax.

The ordeal ended when I could escape to my bedroom, strip off my floor-length gown, throw on a pair of pajamas and write torrid love stories where Paul McCartney served as the centerpiece to my sexual fantasies.

"I know what you mean about those dances," John was saying. "I had to attend formals when I was at West Point - hardly relaxed affairs. I hated them."

Let him believe it was that simple. Anyway, he seemed to think I was gorgeous, so why disillusion him with how ugly I had felt? My brother, Andy, was seven years older. Andy was good-looking and confident. He left home when he was eighteen. When he did come home at Christmastime, he burst on the scene with a beautiful girl on his arm, and

then disappeared again in a social whirlwin
parties. I dreaded the holidays when my n
a sympathetic eye in my direction and say '
was that I had nothing lined up for New Yea

Later that night in Montreal, John and
the hotel. The easiness of the city, the cris ...ight air and
the vodka and tonics had made us relaxed. We took off our
clothes and made love.

"I'm sorry," he said afterwards, self-conscious about his
performance. "I'm like a kid in high school. I should have
taken more time. I want to please you."

"It's okay," I said, lighting a cigarette. I inhaled and
thought how strange but fun it was to be in Canada of all
places with a man I didn't know that well.

We made love again, slowly this time. His mustache tick-
led my lips when we kissed. He had beautiful hands and a
gentle touch. Our room was on the top floor. Lights from the
city spread out below.

Afterwards, we walked the streets where vendors dis-
played Moroccan jewelry and scarves; an old man sat
cross-legged and strummed his guitar. I sensed John was
going to love me. It made me feel impatient and careless
with him. I had been rejected by men so many times. Why
should this be different?

I told him about Alan giving me my first break as a staff
writer for a weekly newspaper. I told him Alan and I were
having an affair.

"He has a pot belly and nicotine stained fingers and is
twice my age, but I don't care. He used to be with the Associated Press."

It was as though I wanted John to know he wasn't special.

"I think we'd better go home," John said angrily.

had promised to take me to Quebec the next day.

"Fine." I shrugged. "If that's the way you want it." For once I had met a man who liked me more than I did him. I felt in control.

"I just made love to you and you tell me about another man you may or may not be in love with. What do you expect?"

"I never said I loved him. Why are you so serious?" I asked as we walked a promenade under a star-filled sky.

He stopped. "I am serious about you, Susan."

People around us kept walking. A father held his child's dripping ice cream cone as the mother tenderly wiped the boy's mouth.

"We hardly know each other." I refused to meet his eyes.

"I know you," he said.

"This is what I mean. You are so damn serious! Can't we just have fun?"

"Whatever you say," he said, sarcastic and irritated.

I was giving my anger back to the wrong man. It was John standing in front of me now.

Chapter Three

John took me to Quebec. It was cold. He demanded my attention.

"Susan, why are you dating someone old enough to be your father?" he asked bringing Alan up again.

"I don't know. Maybe because he is a journalist and can help me become a better reporter."

"And an alcoholic, from the way you describe him."

"So he likes scotch. No one is perfect, John. What about you? What about your girlfriends?"

We walked the boardwalk. In the distance above the St. Lawrence River, Quebec City's artillery park overlooked the Plains of Abraham.

For a moment he said nothing. I thought he was ignoring me.

"Sally was a sister of a classmate," he finally said. "Her father was stationed in Germany. She had reddish-blond hair and the longest legs I had ever seen. She reminded me of Rita Hayworth. When I got to Frankfurt, it was snowing. She barely said anything. Then the truth came out. There was this guy, a captain in her father's battalion. She loved him. This after I flew across the Atlantic at Christmas just to be with her."

"After I got back from Germany, I was sick. At first they thought it was the flu. I remember the barium they made me drink. It smelled just like the white chalk dust of my Catholic school days when I would clean the erasers for Sister Mary Vincent.

"Then they diagnosed the colitis and told me they couldn't commission me. Graduation," he shook his head. "Everyone throwing their caps in the air, congratulating each other about assignments to Hawaii and Germany. I grabbed my diploma, got in the car and drove home, back to my teenage bedroom. I ended up in the hospital. They thought I was going to die."

He shrugged. "It doesn't matter now. It's over. Nothing is like it's portrayed in movies – especially love."

I felt a chill run through me, even though the sun was shining off the blue-gray river, making it a ribbon of light. This man could love. This man could love so much it almost killed him.

I laughed to lighten the mood. "My boyfriend in college, the man I thought I loved, turned out to be a closeted homosexual. My competition was a short little man with a Boston accent."

The frown creasing John's brow eased. He smiled as we kept walking along the boardwalk. "Why him?"

"He looked like Mick Jagger. As soon as I saw him, I was hooked. Jackson introduced me to new things - Modigliani,

Indian cuisine, Ingmar Bergman films. He ma
exciting for a while."

"Unlike me. I'm too serious."

I stopped walking. I looked at him. At twe
three years younger than John. I had never bee .....un a real
man. I had never been with a man looking for a commitment.

Sadness and illness were John's companions. Maybe it
was why he didn't smile much. I wanted to reach out and
touch his arm. Something held me back.

I bit my lip. "I want to enjoy my life. There's no sense
dwelling on tragedy."

John's dark eyes shifted from mine. He looked out
toward the river. "Sometimes," he said more to himself than
to me, "it comes your way when you least expect it."

That night we slept in separate beds. I wasn't ready for
more commitment. In the morning John and I didn't talk.
He drove at 80 miles per hour as we headed out of Quebec in
a downpour to make the drive back to Pennsylvania.

"Slow down," I yelled as he took the curves at high speed.
He knew it irritated me. But he ignored me.

"I jumped out of planes when I was at West Point," he
grimly informed me.

"We're not in a plane."

When we got back to my apartment complex, John
gunned the MGB and drove off. He had driven me up to
Canada simply because I said I wanted to go. Yet, all I did was
argue with him, throw another man up in his face and accuse
him of being too serious.

Two weeks after that trip, my best friend, Denise, who
had introduced John and me at Valley Forge, had a party.
John was standing in Denise's dining room.

He was no longer the raging maniac on the highway driving back from Canada. If anything, he seemed nonchalant and at ease. I was upset that he hadn't called. I had missed hearing his voice.

My life seemed dull – like the school board meetings I chronicled in the local newspaper. At night I had caught myself thinking about him; the shape of his hands on the steering wheel, the way his brow furrowed when he concentrated, his kisses gentle but urgent. Now John was standing here. His masculinity radiated toward me.

"Hi." My hand trembled as I reached for a wine glass.

"How have you been? How's life at the newspaper?"

"Fine." My pulse had quickened.

"I saw one of your articles on education. It was good, well written. How's Alan?" His voice held a hint of sarcasm.

"Oh, he's okay. I don't see him anymore. Except at work, of course."

"That's good, I guess," John said.

He walked off. A dark-haired woman began talking to him.

I picked at some food, sipped my wine. I wanted to turn around, look for John, but the old feelings of rejection had kicked in. I was the girl in ninth grade with an outbreak of pimples who never got asked on a date. Then I felt a hand lightly touch my shoulder.

"Do you want to talk?"

I felt as though he had read my thoughts. "Yes. Please."

I invited him back to my apartment for a cup of coffee. We never got to the coffee.

"You're beautiful," he said, his lips buried in my hair. We lay on my bed, my stuffed animals tossed on the floor.

I studied his long dark eyelashes, the dark hair on his arms and chest. "Why didn't you call me?"

"I figured if you wanted to talk to me, you would call. If you didn't, that was that. I'm nobody's doormat."

"I'm sorry I was so mean to you in Canada."

I wanted to tell him I had been afraid, but something held me back. Never reveal too much, at least in the beginning. My father had taught me that.

John pulled me closer. "Would you like to go dancing?" he smiled.

"I don't know how," I said.

"I do. Come here," he answered.

Chapter Four

John told me he grew up in South Philadelphia. His family left the city and moved to Horsham, a suburb of Philadelphia, when he was seventeen. His mother, Louise, came through Ellis Island from Italy when she was seven years old.

John's father, Mike, managed large construction projects. Louise drove to dry cleaners and food stores for John's twenty-six-year-old brother, Michael, who lived at home. John described his parents as "tolerating one another." They didn't divorce because they were Catholic.

Our backgrounds couldn't have been more different.

My father's family came to Philadelphia from Germany prior to the Revolutionary War. Three generations of Weidener men – all named Andrew - had graduated from the University of Pennsylvania. My parents were childhood sweethearts. Gert and Andy grew up across from one another on Maplewood Avenue in Germantown. They had been married going on forty years.

Women's Room changed my life, I told John.

a career and life outside of marriage was
n identity.

glamorous brunette when she was in
a housewife. Her days revolved around
bargain hunting at supermarkets. She didn't go to college, although my father offered to send her after my brother and I were grown. She turned him down. Gertrude suffered from chronic anxiety and obsessive compulsive disorder. If my father was late from work, she paced, worrying it would upset the routine of cocktails and dinner hour.

Mother rarely guided me in the ways of womanhood. The only advice she gave was to try marriage at least once and make sure my legs were shaved and my toenails clipped on my wedding night.

I had already spent much of my life trying not to be like my mother. If anything, my confidence came from my father who told me I was "beautiful and talented" and could be anything I wanted.

After college, I traveled to Europe and then on to the University of Pennsylvania to get my master's degree.

John and I usually met over the lunch hour because it was too hard to wait until the end of the day. We were caught in the thrill, the magic of sex.

"My mother's nickname for me is Toots. I have no idea why," I told him.

He laughed. "It's cute. Come here, Toots."

His silver and gold West Point saber was mounted above an ugly boxy mustard-colored couch in his apartment. The saber was his attempt at interior decorating in an otherwise drab bachelor pad. It was also a reminder of his dream to be a career Army officer that had eluded him because of illness.

Again in a Heartbeat

V. F. academy

I brought bunches of flowers, big red and gold chrysanthemums with green ferns. I arranged them in a crystal bowl on the dining room table to relieve the austerity. I would stand by the window and watch for him to walk up the sidewalk from the academy campus.

I'd hear his footsteps moving up the stairs, lithe and sure. I stripped off his overcoat, then his uniform. He'd quickly unbutton my blouse. We'd move into the bedroom and make love.

For the first time in my life, I did not worry how my body looked. His hands defined me.

"You are my beautiful, blond reporter," he said.

After all the losers - Alan, with the nicotine-stained fingers, Jackson, my closeted homosexual boyfriend – I just lay there breathing. Pure oxygen. Intensely alive.

"I love you," I whispered.

"Love is too weak a word for what I feel - I luuurve you, you know, I loave you, I luff you," John said.

"Annie Hall."

We lay next to each other.

"We ought to get married. Don't you think?" It was out before I knew it.

"What kind of a question is that?" He wasn't smiling. I panicked.

He saw my look. "Hey." He grabbed me and pulled me down on him. "I'm ready if you are. I just wasn't sure you were."

"You're serious... about getting married?" I had moved against him and lay in the crook of his arm.

"I'm serious. Why? Aren't you?"

I realized something wonderful was finally happening in my life. All those years of blind dates, lonely weekends in

21

college, affairs that ended in cynicism and disillusionment, had hardened me. Now my luck had changed.

I looked into his dark eyes. "I'm serious," I said.

He got out of bed. "Come here."

Our bodies were still damp from lovemaking. The sun was shining through the bedroom window, spreading across the hardwood floor like a yellow carpet of light.

"Will you marry me?" he asked.

"Yes. I'm yours. All yours."

"Good. I want all of you."

"You may regret it," I teased.

He smiled. "I don't think so."

It wasn't a surprise solitaire diamond in a champagne glass or a proposal on bended knee. It was us in his bedroom between his classes and my reporting assignments. A stolen lunch break proposal.

His desire to marry me made me feel like the women I had always envied; the girls in high school who wore their boyfriend's class ring and went to the senior prom while I stayed at home, dreaming about Paul McCartney.

When I was a little girl my father had held me up in the water above the roaring cauldron of ocean.

"Take me out to the hair combers, Daddy," I shouted.

Dad laughed. He held me tighter. "Here comes a big one!" The green and gray waves came at us with a whooshing roar, pushing back my hair. I knew there were sharks and jellyfish out there and people drowned, but I wasn't afraid because my father held me in his strong and loving arms. Now John had come along. With him, I felt safe.

Chapter Five

Two months after the Canada trip, John and I stood near Boathouse Row along the Schuylkill River in Philadelphia. He had bought me a beautiful one-carat diamond ring. He put his arm around me. The sun danced on the river. I held out my hand. The diamond in its yellow gold Tiffany setting reflected prismed colors.

The following weekend we were at a dance at Valley Forge Military Academy. John held me close on the polished floor of Mellon Hall. We had announced our engagement to friends and family and were to be married in June.

"I feel sorry for them," I said, taking John's arm as we watched the lockstep motion of the cadets and their dates.

John smiled. "Bring back memories?"

"Yes, indeed," I laughed. "Memories I would just as soon forget."

We stepped out onto the balcony. A full moon hung white and pure in the sky. John wrapped his arm around my bare shoulders.

"A penny for your thoughts?" he asked.

I turned and smiled. "You're so much better than Paul McCartney."

"Not as rich though."

"But much sexier," I whispered into his ear.

We went back into the ballroom where a Tommy Dorsey band played "Moon River." Cadets approached us to introduce their girlfriends. Chris wanted to attend West Point. John mentored him and the two had developed a close relationship. Chris handed John a small wooden figurine.

"This is for you, sir," he said. "It's Don Quixote. In your classes you get us to think about things and then encourage us to speak our minds. None of the other teachers here do that. You're a rebel."

John's nickname in the West Point yearbook was "Easy Rider." Like the main characters in that movie, he had earned a reputation as a freethinker. He told me he had challenged in his classes the notion that the Vietnam War was an honorable one. It didn't earn him many points with the military establishment.

"Thanks, Chris." John studied the slender wooden man with bowl-shaped hat holding a lance. "The knight errant in search of truth. Yet the butt of a cosmic joke."

Chapter Six

After we got engaged and I moved into John's apartment, his mother began phoning. I could hear John in the hallway. "Susan and I are getting married. You can't stop that."

One day I heard voices and looked out the window of our apartment. I saw John standing with Louise in the parking lot. She was screaming and gesticulating. It was another wild explosion we had come to expect on almost a daily basis. When John came upstairs, I asked him what was going on. He said his mother threatened to call the academy dean and get him fired because we were "living in sin."

"She'll calm down," he said.

John said he had become his mother's confidante over the years. His father and brother ignored her.

"She was so lonely, she used to drive to West Point on weekends," John explained. "I told her not to but she showed up anyway. She's jealous of you."

It wasn't long after I met Louise that she began insulting me. "She's from the *Main Line*," she said, making the place sound dirty. She and John's brother, Michael, snickered when they said, "Main Line" and "Main Liners." John would hug me, tell them they were idiots. But underneath the joking, I felt her anger. I noticed her white ankle socks, her old loafers with a hole in the toe. What a comparison to my own mother, who wore high heels and diamond rings!

Although I thought Louise was rude, I was careful and polite whenever we spoke. I had read enough *Psychology Today* articles to figure she had low self esteem. After John and I got engaged, her violent eruptions shocked me. She screamed it was his fault for not being commissioned. She said horrible things to him. "You're not a man," was one of them. Another was, "You have no mind of your own anymore. *She* controls you," meaning me.

John told me she had to drop out of high school to work in her father's South Philadelphia bakery. Every afternoon when John came home from school, Louise was in her usual pose. The ironing board was placed in the center of the small linoleum floored kitchen. The little plastic RCA radio on top of the refrigerator was tuned to the afternoon soap operas and a huge pile of clean laundry was on the floor next to the ironing board.

"She was very young when she understood her dreams would never be realized," John said.

West Point was her dream, too. John would be the first in her family to graduate from college. After the Army refused to commission him, Louise fluctuated between tears and rage – rage at John and rage at the academy. It was always the same; her against the world. She hadn't spoken to her parents or her sisters in years.

When John lived at home after West Point, his colitis flared up and he had to be hospitalized for internal bleeding. Louise nursed him back to health, only to try to destroy his well-being after he began dating. No one was ever good enough and everyone had a hidden agenda.

John's father drowned his depression in Crown Royal, but never divorced Louise out of Catholic guilt.

John said his father had a reputation as a tough guy on the job. His workers called him "Big Mike." John said "Big Mike" wilted when Louise yelled at him. Most of the time, John's father took assignments in towns and cities where he would be gone for months. He sent Louise his paychecks.

Her rage intensified the closer we got to the wedding. That's when the hang up calls started. Whenever I answered the phone, Louise hung up. Almost immediately, it started ringing again. When John answered, I could hear her screaming even though he was in the hallway and I was in the living room. I worried that John would get sick from the stress.

Our wedding was set for June. It was 1978. Jimmy Carter was president. The *Deer Hunter* won the Academy Award for best picture. And I was dealing with Louise, the future mother-in-law from hell.

How she had produced this wonderful, kind and educated man soon to be my husband was beyond my comprehension. His gentleness and attempts to excuse his mother's behavior were heartbreaking.

John and I met Big Mike one night for dinner. He was heading out on a three-month assignment in North Carolina to oversee the construction of a shopping mall.

We sat in the small Chinese restaurant with a view of the busy highway. His sad blue eyes behind glasses spoke of a beleaguered man.

"I'm sorry about the hang-up calls," he said, shaking his head. "That woman . . . She calls me a drunk. Maybe I am. I drink Crown Royal so I don't have to listen to her. I never did a goddamn thing right in my life, according to her."

He reached into his back pocket, pulled out his wallet and handed John two one hundred dollar bills.

John pushed the money away. "No, Dad."

"Take it." Mike's voice was brusque. A cigar was clenched tightly between his teeth. "Go buy Susan something nice. I know you don't make shit on a teacher's salary."

We said goodbye in the parking lot. After Mike drove away, John shook his head in disgust. "He always gives me money. He never had much to say in the way of advice."

Chapter Seven

A few days after that dinner, John and I were finishing lunch at his apartment when the pounding on the front door started. I stiffened. It was twelve-thirty and John had to teach a class at one o'clock. I was due back in the office to finish interviewing a township supervisor.

John opened the door.

"Look at you with your whore," Louise screeched.

A band of gray roots stood out against her dyed jet-black hair, giving her a hag's appearance. Louise's long tan, cashmere coat hung loosely on her bony frame.

She ripped John's West Point saber off its mounting on the wall. "This is mine," she said holding the saber like a crazed general refusing to admit defeat. "I earned it, not you. Stay with your whore. You're no son of mine," she screamed.

John seemed calm. He stood six feet tall and towered over her. "Mom. Stop it. Please."

Ignoring him, she stepped toward me. "You," she sneered.

"Leave us alone," I shouted. I felt the challenge from her and responded as much for myself as for John.

She lunged. When I put my hand out in self-defense, the tip of the saber went through the soft flesh between my thumb and forefinger like butter. There was no pain.

"You're no West Pointer," she screamed at John as I held my stinging hand in shock. "You're a loser!"

Sharp and effortless as a surgeon's scalpel, the sword had gone clean through my hand.

With that final invective, she was done, her rage spent. John got her out of the apartment, down the stairs to the front door. He came back, pulled me against his chest.

"Oh, sweetheart, I am so sorry."

I could see he was near tears. "Let me look at your hand," he said.

I was trembling. There was no blood, just a tiny purple gash. I felt no pain.

"That's it," he said firmly. "I'm done with her."

The doctor pronounced me lucky that the saber had missed a tendon. When he asked if I planned on filing a police report, I said I loved John. She was his mother. I also knew stress could cause another flare up of John's colitis. I sensed his illness had roots in his childhood.

My minister suggested we immediately get married in a civil ceremony. That way, we could simply announce that we were husband and wife and there was nothing Louise could do.

By the time of our church wedding on June 17, 1978, we had been married a month. No one but Denise and my parents knew. My parents hired a security guard to patrol the church grounds. Although we had invited him, John's father stayed away.

Our reception was held at an old Victorian mansion on the Main Line with wrought-iron gates. It was overcast and I watched the sky, hoping the sun would break through the clouds. But it never did.

The mauve rhododendron in the outside courtyard of the mansion was in bloom. John and I greeted our small circle of family and friends.

"They're playing our song," John said, as we went indoors for our first dance as husband and wife.

He held me close, his hand cupping mine against his chest as we danced to "As Time Goes By." *Casablanca* was John's favorite movie.

Our gold wedding rings caught the light as we held hands and moved in rhythm to the music.

He pulled back and took me in. "Here's looking at you, kid." I knew he was thinking of *Casablanca.*

He could recite by heart the farewell scene between Bogie and Bergman. *"If that plane leaves the ground and you're not on it, you'll regret it. Maybe not today. Maybe not tomorrow. But soon and for the rest of your life."*

John loved the twist of tragedy and the irony of that story. He admired Bogie's heroism - of letting the woman he loved go because it was the honorable thing to do. It was Bergman I felt sorry for – she had no choice but to say goodbye to the man she loved.

In the hotel after the wedding reception, we ordered BLT's. We were ravenous.

"I waited all day to get you alone," my husband whispered in my ear.

"Well, now you have me," I laughed.

One of those old black and white films where the men and women were downing cocktails was on TV. Everyone was unhappy and cynical about life. Despite an inauspicious beginning, the bad stuff in movies was just that. I had lived a sheltered life.

I reached over to John and held his hand. In the morning we were leaving for a honeymoon. Both of us loved New England and the ocean. It seemed impossible to believe that barely a year after meeting John Cavalieri, I was his wife.

Five years would pass before John spoke to his mother. By then, we were expecting our son, Alex. I made John promise he would never leave our child alone with her.

Chapter Eight

On the first anniversary of our trip to Canada, John gave me one long-stemmed red rose. *"One year, one rose,"* he wrote on a note card. *"Love Forever."*

He liked to grab me in the kitchen while we were making dinner. As the pasta simmered and the aroma of garlic and tomatoes merged in the air, he pulled me into the living room.

"Shall we?" John said. We began dancing cheek-to-cheek. Sinatra crooned *"Fly me to the moon and let me play among the stars."* Outside, it was dark and cold.

All men paled in comparison to him: his wit, his sexiness, his desire to be with me. Had there ever been another life before this?

We moved to New Jersey in August 1978. He had taken a position teaching calculus at a public high school. It paid twice the salary at Valley Forge Military Academy.

I applied for a reporting job at the *Princeton Packet*, a weekly newspaper, but didn't get it. Without work, I'd go to the mall, wander aimlessly. The high point of my day was smoking cigarettes and waiting for John to come home so I could vent my frustration.

I resented that he had a job, a chance to use his skills and talents and I didn't. I needed to work, to bring home a paycheck. John didn't care that I was unemployed, but I felt useless.

"I could have gone back to Europe if I hadn't married you!" I shouted when he got home from work. "Crete, the ruins, the Aegean, the best tomatoes and olives I ever ate. Well, those days are over. Instead, I end up in New Jersey!"

He went into the kitchen, poured himself a stiff Jack Daniels.

"Well?" I shouted at him.

He came out of the kitchen. "Well, what, Susan? What do you want me to say? That instead of the Aegean all I can offer you is the Delaware River a mile down the road?"

"Never mind. Just forget it, John!"

He was growing his hair long for me. It turned up at the collar. I was trying to rid him of the stiff military look of his West Point days.

He sat down on the sofa next to me. "You'll get a job," he said putting his hand on my knee. Slowly he ran it up my thigh.

"Right," I huffed. My skin shivered from his touch.

"I'll tell you what," he said. "I'll quit this job at the end of the school year. We'll go back to Pennsylvania. Maybe you can get your old job back as a reporter."

"And work for Alan? No thanks."

But the fact that he was offering to change his life for me made me love him even more. I took his hand and led him into the bedroom.

A month later, I was hired as a substitute English teacher at a nearby high school. I loved teaching *The Great Gatsby*. Some of the girls sat in the back of the classroom, filing their fingernails. Who cared if they didn't appreciate the romance symbolized by the green light at the end of Daisy's dock? I had a paycheck again. I felt like the woman John wanted, not a housewife.

On weekends John and I drove along the Delaware River to New Hope. We visited artsy shops permeated with the pungent odor of burning incense and lavender soap. We drank ice cold beer at a pub overlooking a canal where ducks and swans glided over dark green water.

That October John and I drove to West Point for a football game. He took me down to Flirtation Walk, a winding gravel and dirt path which follows a circuitous route through thick woods beside the shore of the Hudson River. Halfway along the path is a huge rock, nicknamed Kissing Rock. The legend goes, John said, that a girl has to let her cadet escort kiss her under the rock or it will promptly fall on their heads.

"The fact that the rock has stood here for over one hundred years is testament to some very gullible women or a very weak legend," he joked.

It was along Flirtation Walk that nineteen-year-old John Cavalieri lost his "cherry," cadet slang for virginity.

"I remember that when I reached down and started to fumble with my zipper, tiny soft white fingers were there to assist me. That's when I realized that Mary was no novice at this."

I had already told him about my first time. I just wanted to get it over with. I was a junior at American University. Stoned, we ended up on a mattress on the floor. He rode a motorcycle and had long dark hair which he pulled into a pony tail. He stayed until morning. I watched as he drove off with a jaunty wave. Washington had been a pit stop on a road trip he planned all the way to California.

"At least you remember her name," I laughed.

Now as John and I stood under Kissing Rock, my husband pulled me to him. "Come here, Mrs. Cavalieri. Can't let the rock fall on our heads."

Chapter Nine

In November we went to an Army Navy party. "You were the prettiest woman there," he told me when we got home. "All night I kept thinking how I would love to have your long legs wrapped around me."

"Stop," I giggled, feeling self-conscious. But it was good to feel that laugh inside of me.

"Let's make love." He had already started unbuttoning his shirt. "Stop giggling or I'll tickle you."

"It's late," I smiled. I knew I wanted to make love to him, too. I had been thinking the same thing at the party.

John loved sex and romance. He entered West Point a naïve parochial-educated boy, still a virgin. His unfamiliarity with women continued until West Point and then the disastrous affair with Sally. I was the first woman who truly loved him.

On my birthday card the following July, he wrote, "To someone who has become my alter ego and my better half.

You have made all my dreams come true – and then some. Don't stop now."

I had grown up on the cloistered Valley Forge Military Academy campus where every morning I listened to reveille and every evening to Taps. I dreamed of becoming a famous novelist one day. I read *Gone with the Wind* and Kathleen Winsor's *Forever Amber.* I had been an ordinary girl yearning for a life outside those gates of my home. Now I had found one. I had a best friend, lover and husband wrapped up in one gorgeous man.

That following year as John promised, he quit the job in New Jersey and took a job at Lower Merion High School outside of Philadelphia. We moved to an apartment complex in Malvern, a town in Chester County.

I was hired as a reporter for the weekly newspaper, *The Main Line Times.* Once again I covered school board and township meetings. This time I got to write an opinion column. I wrote about the death of John Lennon, the need for passage of the Equal Rights Amendment and memories of Christmas. I got to interview Leonard Nimoy - *Star Trek's* Mr. Spock – when he visited Villanova University.

Between journalism and my marriage, life was fun. Unlike me, John could be totally uninhibited. We'd go to parties and John imitated Travolta in *Saturday Night Fever* strutting and twirling, even doing a split at the end of the dance. That always brought a few "ouches." John had a kind of cocksure confidence and enjoyed being the center of attention. I was the envy of many women.

In the summer of 1981 John and I took a vacation to California, the first time either of us had been there. We stood under the piercing blue skies and looked up at El Capitan. I reached for his hand and our fingers interlaced. Yosemite was a bright rocky landscape of orange and yellow. Then we drove the Coast Highway to Los Angeles. It was my first introduction to the West and the beginning of a love affair with that incredible landscape that would last a lifetime.

We played a game after that.

"Best meal ever," John prompted me.

"The Blue Moon Saloon, Redondo Beach," I automatically responded.

"Seals sunbathing on the rocks," John said with a smile.

"We could see them from the windows of the restaurant," I finished.

There were days when I sensed the depression with what he called "the beast," meaning the ulcerative colitis. Despite his best efforts, he never really got the disease under control.

Chapter Ten

On October 1, 1983, Alex Weidener Cavalieri, was born. John was the first person to hold him. Father and son looked into each other's eyes and in that moment I knew a deep level of happiness. Then John made a strange comment.

"I don't want him to make the same mistakes I did."

"Not being commissioned wasn't your fault."

"Maybe." He squared his shoulders and gave Alex back to me. "All I know is that my son needs to be tougher than I was."

Some nights John stayed up until two or three in the morning, building tiny villages and towns on a model train platform in the basement and smoking imported cigars. I sensed he needed the time alone. West Point and the disappointment of being rejected by the military never relinquished its hold on him.

John changed diapers, heated formula and fed his baby son. As our child grew, he set up a tent in the basement where Alex could play with his Superhero figures. Alex talked to Batman or the Joker inside the tent, his little knees drawn up to his chest. He got so involved he didn't want to come out of the tent.

John bragged about Alex to people at work.

"Susan and I are convinced the kid is a genius. He puts a puzzle together faster than I do and he's only three."

Alex looked like John. He had inherited none of my characteristics of light hair and blue eyes.

Once I got shampoo in Alex's eyes. After that he screamed and fought whenever I tried to wash and rinse his hair. His stubbornness at having things his own way was more than I could handle after a day at work. I lost my temper and wondered what I was doing wrong. I was thirty-three when Alex was born. There was no question it was hard making adjustments when you waited past thirty to have a baby.

Still, I was fascinated with my child. I loved being a mother. Every night Alex begged me to read him a story. We cuddled in bed as I read Disney books. His favorite story was *Sleeping Beauty*. Alex was fascinated with the wicked fairy godmother Maleficent and how she transformed into a monstrous purple and green dragon.

John had left teaching for the computer science field. Both of us worked for Burroughs – which later became Unisys. I was a technical writer. I loved reporting, but night meetings and a baby didn't mix so I made the decision to leave journalism. It was one I soon regretted. Technical writing was so boring it felt like I put my brain in a drawer at eight-thirty and took it out again at four-thirty.

When I was a reporter, the comments were usually the same: "Wow, that must be a very exciting job," or "What kind of stories do you write?"

People were impressed when I said I interviewed Bob Hope and Leonard Nimoy. Now the conversation fell flat. Technical writing interested no one, least of all me.

Still, I was happy to have the job. The second income bought us some breathing room. Often when I was with John I would hear a voice inside me whispering, "You are too happy. This won't last."

Life went on and John got promoted to manager. By 1986 we had truly entered middle-class America. We had bought a large three-bedroom townhouse in Frazer, had a three-year-old son we were convinced was a genius and planned to have a second child.

We ushered in 1987 watching *Electric Horseman,* a tale of love between a broken down rodeo champion and an uptight reporter with an ambitious agenda. Afterwards, we cranked up the music, blasting "My Heroes Have Always Been Cowboys," which Willie Nelson sang in the movie.

After the movie, John came into the bedroom. He looked tired, dark circles under his eyes. I figured too much partying on New Year's Eve. He had a beautiful body. His stomach muscles were flat and taut. He took his time. I opened in his embrace. That night we had made a baby.

A couple of weeks later, we got the home pregnancy kit. We watched that strip of paper turn blue. Positive! It was our introduction to our son, Daniel.

We hugged in the bathroom. What was an otherwise unattractive tableau outside the window of our townhome was saved by one small dogwood tree on our little plot of front lawn. Its thin branches were dark against the winter backdrop of white sky.

"I can still see you that first time we met, standing under the dogwood trees at the school," I said.

John smiled. "It seems like the bonds just strengthen between us with each passing year."

"Now we are expecting another baby," I said.

"Alex is going to have a little brother or sister."

"Thank you," I whispered in his ear.

"I can't live without you. I don't know if that is good or bad, but it is the way it is," John said. "I love you."

I kissed him. I looked into his kind brown eyes. "Tell me again," I urged.

"I love you," he said, holding me tight.

That was six months before the enemy entered our lives and took up residence.

Chapter Eleven

Pregnancy was much easier the second time around. With Alex, I had been sick for almost four months. This time I felt really fine, very strong and healthy.

John and I had decided that as soon as the next baby was born, we would sell the townhouse and buy a single-family home. I'd had amniocentesis and we knew the baby was another boy. It seemed right that the brothers should have their own backyard.

John got a promotion. Life was good, except John was feeling tired.

"It's probably nothing," he said.

I was editing a manufacturing systems manual when I got the call at work. On my desk was a book of baby names. I had surreptitiously been thumbing through it. I liked "Daniel" because it sounded manly, yet eloquent. John wanted the baby to have his name, but I felt it would strip him of his own identity.

John bowed to my desire. "Whatever you wish," he said.

"Hi, honey," I said when I heard his voice at the other end of the phone that day at work.

"How are you, babe?" he asked.

I was thinking how much I wanted to see him later after work. We would go home, give Alex dinner and read him a story. After Alex was asleep, John and I would share our day.

"I'm good. What about you? How did it go at the doctor's?"

"I need to see you," he said.

He was sitting alone when I walked into the Caboose, an actual Pennsylvania Railroad car set on tracks that had been converted into a restaurant in Strafford.

I heard the music . . . "A Whiter Shade of Pale." It was the summer of 1967 again. I was back in my bedroom, a seventeen-year-old girl, dreaming of falling in love someday – innocent and hopeful.

Did his hand brush at his eyes when I walked into the restaurant? Had he been crying? He ran a hand nervously through his thick dark hair.

"Hi, babe. Do you want a drink?"

"You know I can't drink," I said, feeling the baby kick. I swallowed. I was scared.

"It seems there was a little problem."

He smiled and grabbed my hand. His eyes filled with tears.

"Ah, well, the doctor thinks I have cancer."

I felt the blood drain from my face.

"The doctor wants me admitted to the hospital and have surgery right away, but forget that. I have to think about this," John said.

It seemed the colitis – the "beast" that had derailed John's Army career - had now veered off into a full-blown attempt to kill him.

Wednesday, June 17, 1987, was our ninth wedding anniversary, two days from now.

I swallowed. I found my voice. "Is he sure? Suppose the test is wrong? This can't be happening now. This isn't fair."

The horrifying news that my husband had just been diagnosed with colon cancer was not to be believed. We had a three-year-old child, another one on the way; we had a life that was moving forward. This was unacceptable. It couldn't be true. *I* wouldn't allow it to be true.

"I've got to go. I've got to go home."

I stood up quickly and my chair flew out behind me and went crashing to the floor. I ran out into the sun-filled late afternoon. I fumbled in my purse for my car keys. Tears blinded me. No! No!

John came home that night filled with bravado. The cancer, he said, was no different than the enemy in wartime. He had been taught how to fight the enemy. He would take his training and use it.

"I can beat this. Besides," he said with a smile, "I've got to get ready for that new little boy of ours."

I felt anger rise in my chest. "Where is the joy in having a new baby when you've done something incredibly stupid like get sick?"

With that I ran up to the bedroom and slammed the door. I was shaking. I recognized his bravado for what it was. I lay down on the bed and pulled the covers over me. I wished I had never met him. He was being stolen from me. Cancer is a thief.

Only later did he come upstairs. I could see the exhaustion in his face. He crawled under the covers.

"I'm sorry. I didn't want you upset."

"How kind of you," I said. I rolled over, my back to him.

His apology just made me feel more ashamed. I hated myself at that moment. That's what cancer does to you. It divides your house. That's why John called it the enemy.

Chapter Twelve

The mood in our house was somber. There was no joking and there were long periods of silence. John and I tried to keep up with things as usual for Alex. We read articles on second opinions and how to avoid unnecessary surgery.

A CT scan had shown a tumor that looked like it had spread out of John's intestine but the extent of it was not known. Three surgeons wanted to do radical surgery – a colostomy. John wanted to avoid that if he could but our research was not encouraging. Colorectal cancer was one of the greatest killers among men.

Finally, we had one last hope. After weeks of searching around the Philadelphia area, we found a surgeon at Bryn Mawr; the hospital where I had been born and where Alex had been born.

By now it was early July. John was not in any pain, but his weight was down ten pounds. The doctor's office was tiny and decorated with no particular theme or period. In fact, cluttered might be an apt description.

Dr. Tom Wayne jumped up to greet us. He seemed energetic and bouncy. He had an aura of confidence without the cockiness. He showed John into a small examining room. Shortly, he and John returned.

"First off, call me Tom," he said. "I can get the tumor out."

"Yes, I know, we've heard the whole colostomy routine," John said.

"No, no, I mean I can get it out and save your life and keep the damage down to a minimum."

These were the magic words John and I had been waiting to hear.

The doctor took out a pad and began drawing a diagram. Although the tumor was low, there was just enough room to cut out the bad section of John's colon and reattach it.

"Every other doctor has suggested a total colostomy," John said.

Tom's eyes narrowed but his tone stayed upbeat and cheery.

"I would recommend a colostomy, too, if you agreed. But part of the success of any operation is the patient's attitude. If you don't want a colostomy, then the whole procedure could be a psychological disaster."

I noticed for the first time that his hands looked soft and tiny. I tried to picture him probing John's insides.

As we got up to leave, Wayne left us with one cautionary reminder.

"Just remember. Cancer is not a simple disease."

The day I drove John to Bryn Mawr Hospital for his surgery, we were upbeat. John had undergone radiation in the weeks before to shrink the tumor and now we were ready to kill the cancer once and for all. John checked in at the administration office and answered a barrage of bureaucratic questions and signed myriad release forms.

There was no time for long farewells.

"I'll call you later," he said. "You head on home."

The next day, Friday, dawned. I arrived at the hospital early. John and I sat quietly, holding hands and talking inanities. Sometime that morning John had an EKG done and more blood drawn. Dr. Wayne showed up around noon and again was bright and cheery and quite positive.

"Ok, tiger, ready to go?" he said to John.

John forced a smile. "Do I have a choice?"

Later that afternoon, I watched as John was wheeled down the hallway under bright lights. I smiled, but I knew I was crying. Then John disappeared behind the operating room door.

The morning after the operation, I entered his room. John was in terrible pain. He had a catheter to keep his kidneys working and drainage tubes on both his right side protruding from his waist and another smaller one in his left abdomen. I reached over to kiss my husband, but he turned away. Later, he would tell me it was because he felt so weak and unattractive. But at that moment, it felt like a horrible rejection.

All I wanted to do was touch him. I sat on the bed and the sudden shift of my weight caused John's body to lurch to the right. He screamed in pain.

"Get off the bed."

I jumped up and started to cry.

"I'll go home now. Call me later. I love you."

My husband was so sick I knew I had to keep it all together back at the house or everything would fall apart. I drove Alex to daycare and kept going to work. I don't remember much of those days... it is all pretty much a black void now.

Chapter Thirteen

While the surgery had gone well – five hours' worth - the lymph nodes were another matter. Thirty-five out of thirty-eight lymph nodes removed were found to be malignant. This news was a major setback.

The warning bells should have gone off in my brain, but I was still in denial. This happened to people who were in their seventies or eighties, not thirty-nine-year-olds like John. One oncologist gave John a fifty percent chance of making it through the first year.

"The hell with statistics," John said.

Although no one had offered him a cure, John acted as though we would beat this monster. I needed to believe him. I had to stay healthy for the baby. Whatever fears consumed him, I rarely saw them. His strength and the combat training that had prepared him to treat cancer no differently than to fight an enemy in the trenches protected our family.

A month later, I was cutting up carrots and celery for vegetable platters the morning of his fortieth birthday party when I went into labor. I looked outside the family room window to see John pull up in our little gray Toyota Tercel.

He had just returned from his chemotherapy treatment.

"I ran track, hiked miles in the heat with a forty-pound ruck sack. I've been on all-night patrols and gone days without sleep, but I have never known exhaustion like this," he told me after the radiation treatments prior to his surgery. Now the chemotherapy had further depleted his compromised and weakened immune system.

He got out of the car. He paused - looked at the small walkway of steps from the car to our front door where a Halloween witch hung at a crazy angle. His face was weary. I wondered if he was measuring the distance from the car to the house. Did he have the stamina to make even that short walk?

A few years ago he had swept up the New York Interstate in a dark green MGB sports car with a high-strung blond who just wanted to go to Canada and have fun. Now he stood, a physical wreck, reduced to driving the proverbial safe car.

He made it up the walk. John opened the front door. His long eyelashes were gone – the chemotherapy had seen to that – but his hair was as dark and thick as ever, except for a silver patch at his temple.

I stepped into the foyer to meet him. He kissed me. I took his hand. It was warm and his fingers firm as they interlaced with mine.

"Well, the baby's not due for another three weeks, but it seems Daniel has his own ideas," I said trying to put a lilt in my voice. "I think he wants to have the same birthday as his father."

John's grin was pure pleasure. "Are you ok?"

"I'm fabulous. He's three weeks early and I'm ready to go to the hospital and have this baby."

"Talk about a fantastic birthday present. You're a pretty amazing woman." He hugged me.

I rested my head on his chest. I could hear his heart beating strong and sure.

We decided it was too late to cancel the party. I called Denise, who we had made Alex's godmother. She said she would pick up the cake and party platters and get Alex from pre-school.

We left the house at noon. At 4:12 p.m. Daniel John Cavalieri was born at Bryn Mawr Hospital.

The birth of our son on September 11, 1987 - John's fortieth birthday - was a remarkable gift. As we gazed at Daniel's sleeping face, I knew that ours was not to question why.

Unlike Alex's birth four years earlier, this time John and I were both more relaxed. My doctor called Daniel our "miracle baby" because we had conceived him right under the wire. The cancer, the surgery, the radiation and now the chemotherapy had made John sterile.

Daniel arrived quiet and reserved, due probably to the epidural, unlike Alex, who came out kicking and screaming after natural childbirth. John held Daniel in the delivery room and looked into his son's eyes.

"It's like he knows me," John said.

For the first time in months, I think both of us felt full of life's energy.

The doctor told me that I could leave the hospital with Daniel and come home for the party, but I wanted to stay there, hold my new son. I studied Daniel's little hand. His fingers were miniatures of his father's beautiful long fingers.

John and I are good people, I thought as I cradled our baby. Our boys need a father to put together a new toy and carry them on his shoulders.

Waiting at home was the thief that was cancer, trying to rob my family of its heart and soul. It wanted the man who one morning before we headed out to work placed a blue velvet box on my dresser. That night when I opened it, there was an opal ring with pale pink and peach glints of light I had admired in a shop window the weekend before.

"You shouldn't have!"

"Of course, I should have." He slipped the ring on my finger. "Not every man is as lucky as I am to have a beautiful wife. I love you, Toots."

Now we had another son, born on his father's birthday. Would Daniel and John celebrate together for years to come? Or would the thief deny them a future?

John headed home from the hospital for his birthday party. He was greeted with drinks and raucous choruses of "Get that man a drink!" John shook hands and passed around cigars.

Denise told me he was so exhausted, he quietly excused himself and went up to bed before the guests left.

The next morning John arrived at the hospital with yellow roses. He looked better – in a tan sports coat and turquoise tinted sunglasses. He had a face like a true Roman. This wonderful warrior was my husband.

Chapter Fourteen

We brought Daniel home from the hospital. Daniel had jaundice because he had been born three weeks early. Our pediatrician told us to keep him in the sunlight.

John spread a baby blanket on the floor by the sliding glass door in our living room. We unsnapped the top to Daniel's turquoise terrycloth pajamas. As the sun shone on our sleeping child, his tiny chest gradually turned from yellow to pink.

"He's beautiful. Thank you," John said kissing my lips.

Neither of us spoke for a minute.

"We will never come this way again," John said.

John became whiter than white from the chemotherapy. To top it all off, he felt sick three weeks out of four – two weeks after the treatment and the week before in anticipation of the next one. That left him one good week to recover.

I felt lonely and undesirable. The man who brought me roses and whose sexual prowess brought out my own passionate nature had withdrawn behind a curtain of illness. Not only had the surgery left John sterile, but his ability to perform sexually had been irreparably damaged. My dream of painting the third bedroom pink was gone.

At night John sat alone in front of the television, not wanting to talk. Then he fell asleep on the couch. I missed the company and conversation of my best friend and confidante.

I sat in traffic jams on my way home from work. I had a strange desire to start driving west toward California. I was on the emotional edge.

Daniel needed to be baptized, so John and I drove to the Church of the Holy Trinity, a soaring contemporary structure in Chester County. Alex had been baptized there. While John was raised Catholic and I, Presbyterian, we agreed the Episcopal Church was a good meeting ground. We also liked that Episcopalians took liberal positions on social issues.

The old priest who performed Alex's baptism had since retired and a new one took his place. We met Father Todd in his office on a bleak November morning.

The office had unadorned gray walls, a blue sofa and two chairs facing a desk. A window looking out on the church's huge, asphalt-paved parking lot completed the dreary scene.

John and I sat in the chairs facing Father Todd Martin, who sat behind the mahogany desk. Scribbled notes lay scattered on the desk near the Bible.

"Sorry for the mess," he said. "I'm working on Sunday's sermon. I'm way behind."

He leaned back in his chair. His black cleric's shirt stretched across his broad chest. He had thick, brown hair and a chiseled jaw. If Father Todd Martin had been a woman, people would have called him a knockout. Years later I realized he looked like John Edwards, the politician.

Father Todd and his wife, Alice, had come to Holy Trinity from a small Kentucky parish. Anxious to know the families that made up Holy Trinity, Father Todd took over baptismal duties.

Father Todd smiled. "I spoke to Father Mike and I understand, John, you have been battling cancer. And now with a newborn, that just makes things harder, puts more of a strain on your marriage, your belief in the Lord."

I could see John sit up defensively. His brow tightened.

"I think Susan and I are well aware of how tough it has been. She was six months pregnant when I was diagnosed. What is important is that Susan and I love each other. We love our sons. We are going to make it through this, God willing."

Father Todd nodded. "However, it is important to truly accept Jesus as our Lord and Savior. This is not something we as Christians can take lightly. It makes sense to take time to pray before we go ahead."

Father Todd's hand rested next to the big Bible on his desk.

"I was raised Catholic," John said. "If you're asking if I have doubts, especially because of my illness, well of course. I've often wondered, why me? But I always felt the answers would come in time through prayer and contemplation."

Father Todd turned his attention to me. "Susan. What about you?"

"I guess you could call me a doubting Thomas," I said. "For one, I never understood the Immaculate Conception beyond the obvious symbolism."

Father Todd leaned back in his chair, satisfied.

"I think by the end of February, we should be ready to baptize little Daniel. That gives us time to talk about Scripture and the Lord's purpose in your lives. Is that alright with you two?"

His blue eyes settled on me, lingered. My heart beat faster. I wondered if he had this effect on all women, simply by virtue of how incredibly handsome he was.

"It's fine with me, if my husband agrees. Is that okay with you, sweetheart?"

I knew the look on John's face. It took all his control to hide the scorn he felt for this man.

John nodded. "Of course. That way we can read the Bible every night."

If he heard the sarcasm in John's voice, Father Todd gave no hint.

He walked us to the door. "By the way, we're starting an evangelical outreach group, visiting people in their homes, spreading the Lord's Good News; the gift of grace is through faith, not good works. Susan, I understand you used to be a reporter. Perhaps, with your excellent communication skills, you would be interested in joining our group?"

I felt a flush rise up my throat from his flattery. "I'll think about it."

When we got home, John fluctuated between anger and amusement. "Where did they find him? Evangelical outreach? Elmer Gantry to the rescue. And by the way, he has no right to tell us we have to wait to baptize our son."

John picked up the phone and called Father Peter, a former Catholic priest who came to Holy Trinity after he married. John admired Peter, a Jesuit and accomplished theologian, now an Episcopalian.

"Who is this guy, Todd, anyway?" I heard John say.

After a brief conversation, John hung up. "It seems Holy Trinity is going through some sort of split – the conservatives want more of a say; they're worried about the move to ordain homosexuals. So they hired Todd, who is a fundamentalist. Peter said he's harmless."

I found myself looking forward to my "spiritual" sessions with Father Todd. Together we talked about Jesus, my doubts, my fear that John was dying.

Father Todd listened. His enjoyment of my company – his compliments that I was strong and intelligent – helped ease the fear of being left alone to raise two children without a husband.

Father Todd's sermons in church were often so simplistic, John would stifle a groan.

"The man's a dolt," John whispered when Todd finished at the pulpit. "Metaphor is beyond him."

At night John closed the door to the study or watched old movies. I sat alone in our bedroom, wondering how it had all come to this. I craved my husband's attention and affection, but found myself thinking about Todd's nod to me that morning in church.

Around church Todd's wife, Alice, was best known for organizing crafts fairs. Her specialty was Christmas tree ornaments. They looked like birds nests with words from Scripture printed on tiny rolled paper and placed like eggs inside the nest.

When she and her husband were together, they acted almost like brother and sister. Neither touched the other. Maybe he doesn't love her, crossed my mind more than once. Maybe it is just a marriage of convenience.

Some nights when I cuddled against John or tried to kiss him, he turned his head. "Don't," he said.

The rejection stung. I ran out of the room, feeling the tears fill my eyes.

His sickness overpowered all else. He had lost over fifteen pounds from the chemotherapy. His legs looked like hairy sticks, all the muscle from running track at West Point, gone.

In February, I watched Father Todd hold Daniel and gently dip my son's head in the font's baptismal water. Afterwards, John and I invited everyone back to our house for coffee and cake. Denise, my parents, and Mark, John's best friend at work and Daniel's godfather, milled together in the dining room. John and Father Todd were cordial but avoided conversation.

I walked Father Todd to the front door.

"You have a beautiful family, Susan. Thank you for letting me be a part of your special day. The Lord be with you and John and Daniel and Alex."

Believing he had brought me closer to Jesus, I hugged him. "Thank you."

His hand stroked my hair. "You're welcome. I'm here for you."

After the baptism, Father Todd and I continued our private sessions.

"You're a born skeptic," he laughed one day leaning closer toward me as we sat on the sofa in his office with the door closed. "I love how you challenge me!"

His leg touched mine, his chiseled jaw a mere inch from my face as he paged through his Bible for a passage he wanted to cite. I told him how lonely I was since John had withdrawn.

He shook his head. "John," he said, "is a real piece of work."

How to explain why I didn't kick him out of my life right then and there? How to explain my need for attention and adulation? How to explain that cancer had invaded my soul, much as it had invaded John's body?

For nine months I had carried a lump within me – Daniel, our beautiful baby – that was life. Now I carried another lump - only this one was evil – infatuation with a married man and a priest, no less. I was cheating on John as surely as if I had slept with Father Todd.

One morning Father Todd phoned me at work.

"I was thinking about you this morning in the shower. You're such a good writer I was hoping you might help me with my next sermon."

I laughed. "You were showering and thinking of me?"

"I'm not good with words. I have ideas, but when I go to put them on paper, it is hard."

John's words, "The man is a dolt" resonated, but not as strongly as images of me lathering Father Todd's naked body with soap.

It had been five months since that November morning John and I met him. In all that time, John and I had not made love.

My relationship with Father Todd had developed into once-a-week lunches. I'd give him some editing advice after reading his sermons. He listened, nodded, made the corrections. I watched the way he sat relaxed in a chair after taking off his suit coat, his black or tan shirt and white priest's collar accentuating his good looks. I convinced myself I mattered to him, was instrumental in his growth as a priest.

We were having lunch one day at one of the many inns in Chester County claiming George Washington slept there. Lunch had been ordered. Outside the restaurant window, pink magnolia blossoms waved gently in a chilly spring breeze.

"How have you been?" Todd asked.

I looked into his eyes. His hand rested on the white linen tablecloth. Briefly I touched it.

"I've been thinking about you and me," I said.

He straightened up. A shadow of discomfort crossed his face.

I struggled on. "Maybe there could be more between us, more than a priest and his parishioner."

He withdrew his hand from the table. He shook his head. "Susan, I probably should have told you this a long time ago."

He was twenty-one years old and selling vacuum cleaners. He met this man, "a boy just like me," he said, lost in his reverie. They lived together, innocently enough at first. The clatter of silverware, the din of conversation around us receded as my hands began to perspire.

He was consumed with self-loathing. What was wrong with him? How could he want another man? He walked and walked and then Jesus appeared to him. He knew what Jesus wanted – to renounce his sin.

Todd dragged himself to a Bible study and religious retreat where he met a woman who convinced him that Christ was the path to forgiveness. He got accepted to a small divinity school in Tennessee and studied to be an Episcopal priest. That same woman, of course, was now his wife.

"Alice accepts me the way I am, flaws and all," he finished.

The sickness in my stomach settled like a stone, my appetite gone.

"Are you telling me that you are a homosexual?"

"I'm not sure. I pray a lot about it."

Carefully, I placed my napkin on the table. I stood up.

"I'm sorry. I really am. It must be horribly painful for you. I have to go now."

As a fundamentalist Episcopalian, he represented the movement opposed to the ordination of homosexuals. How could he deceive the congregation? How could he exploit my vulnerability when my husband was so sick?

His hypocrisy and self-hatred were almost beyond my comprehension. And his revelation to me was one appropriate only to his own religious confessor. How dare he?

But what about me? I had supped on wine and crab over numerous lunches, pretending I was interested in Jesus - all the while lusting after this man, this poor excuse for a priest while the real man in my life lay at home, possibly dying.

Nine months of chemotherapy finally drew to a close. John had gone into remission and with it came the chance for us to put together the pieces of our marriage.

My misplaced anger at John – not the cancer – and my need for admiration and sex outside my marriage resulted in shame and self-loathing for years. The only blessing was that John never knew.

Chapter Fifteen

O n our tenth wedding anniversary John wrote: *Our lives forever changed on June 17, 1978. We have been through a lot. Some good, some bad, some fun, some sad, but never dull.*

We both wanted to achieve greatness in our lives - the great novelist, the noted warrior, the intellectual statesman. Sometimes, we wonder how we arrived here in 1988 with two kids, a station wagon and careers in computers. I think that we have achieved greatness. Maybe we aren't famous, but we are great. We are great because we round each other out and we have lived life "our way." I think our kids will reflect that.

I know that without you my life would have been empty and a lot duller. I know that after ten years, I need you more than ever. I love you like a bride which you will always be, but also like good California wine. You've gotten better. I think of you today and every day and every hour. Always. Love, John.

By the summer of 1988, Daniel was a chubby toddler, pushing around the patio of our townhouse in his blue and red walker.

John barked orders as he held the video camera.

"Alex, stand next to your brother!"

Eager to please, Alex crouched down and slung an arm around Daniel's shoulders.

Then as I bent to pick up Daniel, I heard John say, "And here is my wife's beautiful ass."

"John!"

He teased me by playing that video on television over and over. The camera slowly panned in on my backside. I turned - Daniel's fat, bare legs encircling my midriff, a scolding, embarrassed look on my face.

I think it made John feel he was giving me something as close to sex as he could. It gave me a chance to flirt again.

When Daniel turned a year old, we put the townhouse on the market and began looking for a single-family home. John found the house in Chester Springs, a pricey suburb in a good school district. I did all the negotiating with the realtor who wanted to make a quick sale.

"Tell the sellers they need to come down $20,000 or we walk," I informed her.

"That's a lot. There's someone else interested in the property. I don't think it is going to work."

"If you don't want to do it, we'll find another realtor willing to put the bid in for us."

That night she called. John gave me the high five.

"Nice work," he smiled.

It was a plain boxy house with cedar siding and a maple tree in the middle of the front yard. Its best feature - a big, flat fenced-in backyard where two little boys could play.

Again in a Heartbeat

In spring, 1989 John planted forsythia bushes along the fence. He labored in the sun, digging one hole after another for the scrawny twigs with green sprouts. Year after year, they grew higher and higher, ushering in the spring with their long yellow branches.

My husband bought me a blond cocker spaniel with a perfect apple-shaped head. We named him Brandy Alexander for my favorite after-dinner drink. He was our baby, a third child. That silly dog chewed and ate rubber squeaker toys and then promptly vomited the whole mess on the tan wall-to-wall carpet.

On Mother's Day, John served me breakfast in bed. On the tray table was a card with a picture of a cocker spaniel.

Susan, I saw this card and thought of you – great – I see cockers and think of my lover. Seriously, you love these "stupid" dogs and besides, it gives me an excuse to write "I love you . . . I love you . . . I love you."

In July, John inflated the plastic turquoise swimming pool. As the boys splashed and played, Brandy lay in the shade of the magnolia tree.

At the end of the summer, we traveled to Venice Beach, California, pushing Daniel in his stroller along the artsy main streets, past buckets of tall red and white gladiolas. This was Alex's time – he was curious about everything, loving the colors and the sights. John and I watched him run up and down the sidewalk, leap up and down under a blue sky.

John stayed in remission although he was often fatigued. Nevertheless, we celebrated by driving to Cape Cod in the summer of 1990. Daniel was turning three years old and Alex seven.

Waves crashed against a craggy hillside sprinkled with yellow flowers. The boys ran to the shoreline in search of shells. John looked away from Alex and Daniel, then back to me. Neither of us spoke. Both of us were thinking the same thing, holding the same hope. He'd be there to watch these two boys grow into men.

"I want to give you everything. You deserve the best," he said.

"I have the best. I've got you, haven't I?"

His apricot shirt emphasized the muscular chest and arms he had developed from steroids to counteract the effects of chemotherapy. He was tanned. He had never looked better.

Two seagulls floated in lazy tandem above the shoreline. We had come to a place where John could sit on steps leading from the beach to the street. I pulled out the camera.

When we got home, I placed the photograph in a gold frame on my dressing table. A slight smile plays around John's lips as he looks out toward the horizon.

Chapter Sixteen

It had been six months since we walked along the sea. Dirty pots and pans, cold lasagna and limp salad covered the kitchen countertops and table. The overhead fluorescent light flickered. I wished we were walking along the beach again.

"He gets people to pay for crap software," John said.

I knew immediately who he was talking about. Almost every night he came home angry with his boss, Dave.

"I have to go in and fix his mess. Half the time it still doesn't work and the customer is out thousands of dollars. He needs to start telling them the truth or I will."

"That company will never change. Dave will never change. You know that," I said.

"I have some principles, Susan. It's about honor. If you take away a man's honor, he has nothing."

"Honor is not going to put food on the table or buy a new ceiling fixture," I snapped back. I stood up to clear the table and stepped on a sharp corner of the dog's rawhide bone.

"Shit!" I rubbed my bare foot. "Chris was right when he gave you that statue. You are Don Quixote tilting at windmills. Do you really think that was smart to argue with him when you are up for promotion?"

John pushed away his half-eaten food and loosened his burgundy necktie.

"Sometimes, I don't think you like me very much. It makes me wonder why you even married me. I'm going upstairs to change."

"Jesus, John. I want more for our boys, a bigger house and opportunities to get into a top college. I want more for you than some dead-end job with a jerk like Dave Johnson telling you what to do. Why do you make things harder than they have to be?" I asked following him down the hallway.

He turned and faced me. "Make things harder? Like the cancer I've put you through? Isn't that what you really mean?"

"Keep your voice down. You'll wake the boys." I did not look at him.

"You haven't answered the question, Susan."

His blood test had shown a slight spike in his CEA levels. The oncologist cautioned this could mean the cancer had spread.

"All right, if you want to know, being married to you has not been a picnic. I'm sick and tired of walking on eggshells every three months while we wait for your test results." I heard my reporter's voice, the tough tone I used with the recalcitrant realtor, the surgeon diagramming my husband's insides and talking about cutting him open . . . so they wouldn't think I was scared.

"Oh, and you think I'm having fun with this?" John said. "If anyone wants to trade bodies and health histories with me, they are more than welcome."

My shoulders sagged. I was so weary I could hardly stand. I had started waking up like clockwork at 2 a.m., my whole body tensed. I knew it wasn't about dirty dishes, money, or his job.

"I have cancer, Susan. That changes things. Money and promotion aren't all they're cracked up to be."

I felt his disdain like a slap. Worse was his use of the present tense.

"You're going to be fine." My voice sounded like it was coming from the end of a tunnel. The darkness of the hallway hid my face.

He stepped forward. Suddenly, he was hugging me. His smell was so familiar, the starch from his collar, the hint of soap. He whispered into my ear.

"You won't let anything happen to me, will you?"

I pulled back and looked at him. For the first time, I saw his fear.

I straightened up and spoke calmly. "Of course not."

I ran my hands down the lapels of his navy suit coat. "We're in this together – an unbeatable duo."

I smiled even as I felt a need to sit down.

He laughed. "I'm glad you're on my side. I wouldn't want your guns trained on me."

"Oh, I think you can take it. You've been putting up with me these many years."

The following week two feet of snow fell. John and the boys built snowmen on the front lawn. Brandy, our almost human buff-colored cocker spaniel, came up with a snow-encrusted snout that covered his black gum drop nose.

John went out and bought a bread maker and a juicer. "I want to try a holistic diet," he said.

It was then I knew he was sick again.

At night as he studied how to make soups and breads without preservatives, we waited. Then in March, 1991, our world crumbled again. More tests revealed the cancer had come back. We had just fought a long battle only to find out that the enemy was not gone but mounting another assault.

My husband began exploring his options. Should he go out on permanent disability? The company had begun lay-offs and he feared that if he didn't get disability, they would find an excuse to fire him.

Although only forty-four years old, John had the stick-thin body of a worn-out, old man, thanks to another round of chemotherapy. From then on, John was a marked man. His boss, Dan Johnson, demoted him.

"I feel like Hester Prynne in the *Scarlet Letter* with a big red "C" on my chest instead of an "A," John said.

His back pain was almost constant despite nine or ten Advil a day and he was easily fatigued and often depressed. "America admires leaders who jog and swim and work out. Big business is no different," John said. "Health is the key. Without it you have no career and no future."

I concentrated on journalism again. Fed up with technical writing, I quit and began freelancing for a daily newspaper in West Chester, the *Daily Local News.*

"You're a good writer," John said. "This makes you happy. You're smiling again."

"Thank you," I said. I felt the onset of a headache like a thundercloud above my head. I was guilty as charged. The work made me happy. Meanwhile, my husband was so sick he could barely stand.

Again in a Heartbeat

In the summer of 1991, I got a job with *The Philadelphia Inquirer*. I interviewed school superintendents, businessmen and domestic violence victims. I reported on suburban subdivisions paving over farmland. The work helped me forget a marriage spiraling into despair.

Chapter Seventeen

"It's not good," Tom Wayne told me on the phone. "The cancer is eating John."

I hung up, walked up the winding staircase to the newsroom. I let myself into the ladies room and lost my lunch. The four and a half years since the first surgery had merely been an armistice, not a surrender.

Later that afternoon I took the elevator to the hospital's fifth floor, the cancer floor – the floor some people never left. John was recuperating from his second surgery. Tom Wayne had opened John up, seen the inoperable tumors and then closed John up again. Wayne had not put a timeline on how long John had.

John lay in bed reading *The Sun Also Rises*. I had brought Alex. He crept over to his father's bedside.

"Hi, Dad." He kissed his father's stubble covered, sunken cheek. "How do you feel?"

"I'm good, son. I'll be better once I get out of here."

Suddenly, Alex started to cry, the sobs heaving his little chest. He shook his head and wiped away the tears with the back of his hand, but the tears still came. I watched as John patted the bed. Alex got up and sat next to his father. John crooked his arm around him.

"What is it, honey?" he asked softly.

Alex hiccupped. "I'm scared. Are you going to die, Dad?"

John and I looked at each other over Alex's thick mat of dark brown hair. I felt faint as I looked at a bag drip colorless liquid into John's arm. The room smelled of chlorine and sickness. A portable toilet was parked next to the bed.

John rubbed Alex's head. "We're all going to die some-day, Alex."

Alex nodded, still sniffling.

"But I can tell you one thing. I'm not going to die today and I'm not going to die tomorrow."

Alex looked up at him and a grin split his tear-streaked face.

"That's good, Dad. I'm sorry I cried."

"Hey." John said. "Look at me."

Alex obediently lifted his head.

"Don't ever let anyone tell you that you're not a man if you cry, okay?"

Alex nodded. "Okay, Dad."

I felt as if I couldn't breathe. I grabbed my purse.

"Here honey," I said, handing Alex some money. "Go get yourself a soda and bag of chips out of the machine."

Alex jumped off the bed. "Thanks, Mom," he said and ran out of the room.

"Hi." John's eyes crinkled in the corners when he smiled. He held out his hand to me. I walked over to his bedside. I kissed his lips.

"What can I do for you?" I asked.

He shook his head and grinned ruefully. "I don't know. How about a new body?"

Neither of us spoke for a minute.

"You look pretty," he said. "I like that color on you. It goes with your eyes," he said, touching the aquamarine blouse I was wearing.

"Did you talk to the doctor? What did he say? How did the surgery go?"

In horror, I realized that the surgeon had not given John the bad news. I concentrated on not letting my gaze waver from his.

"He said everything went fine."

John smiled. He seemed satisfied. "That's good. Did he say when I can come home?"

I nodded. "Yes. Another two days."

He closed his eyes. "Thanks for bringing Alex. I'm tired now. Do you mind if I take a nap?"

I leaned down and gently kissed his forehead, stroked his hair. "I love you," I whispered, but he was already asleep.

Chapter Eighteen

"It's just no good," John said. Our attempt to make love had again failed.

I wanted to hold him, but there was a faint odor about him now. It was medicinal and rotting. I got out of bed. "I'm going to take a shower."

Afterwards, I came back into the bedroom in my terry-cloth robe. I wanted to tell him I loved him; that I always would. But he was gone.

I looked out the window at the afternoon sunlight on the maple tree. Tiny green shoots had started to bud. I thought about fifteen springs ago – the first year of marriage.

A trail led to a field behind our apartment complex in New Jersey. We walked and found a spot behind some hedges. We lay down and made love. Afterwards, John grinned like a teenage boy who had gotten away with illicit sex. "That was fun."

I leaned over and looked at him as he lay in the grass. "We're bad. Someone could have seen us."

"I would have told them I was making love to my wife."

Had it all just been a dream? I buried my face in a bath towel so no one could hear my sobs.

John moved out of our bedroom. His nights were restless and painful so he slept in the study. I lay alone listening to the rumble of the turnpike just over the hill from our subdivision.

The doctors' appointments became more numerous; the oncologist, the surgeon, a holistic "doctor." John started going alone so I wouldn't have to miss work.

Finally, in 1993, John went out on disability from Unisys. He had been sick with cancer when Ronald Reagan was president. He was still sick when Bill Clinton was elected. On the advice of a West Point graduate, John contacted the Veterans Administration. John had contracted ulcerative colitis at the academy and had received an honorable medical discharge. A direct correlation could be made between the colitis and cancer. John began receiving VA benefits.

What could we tell Alex and Daniel? Daddy doesn't go to work anymore because he is sick? He might even be dying?

"If I die, you'll get double my salary. If they let me go, you won't get that," John said. "I have to be thinking ahead, be pragmatic about this. That's why I'm out on disability. They can't fire me."

I ran upstairs to my room and turned on the evening news. Breathe in and breathe out I told myself. He could go into remission again. My denial was complete.

Somehow John held it together. While I was at work, he cooked dinner. He ran errands, picked Alex up at school and took care of Daniel.

"Quitting means dying," he said.

The boys seemed happy doing all the things the other children who didn't have fathers with cancer did. They played Little League and soccer. For that I was grateful. I needed a veneer of normalcy. I had never bargained for this either for me or my family.

My husband no longer went to work and now I knew he never would again. His chemotherapy treatments made him so sick, he had to run to the bathroom in the middle of a conversation to vomit or have diarrhea. Once again, I found myself at the emotional edge.

I gave you the best years of my life! I screamed inside my head. Now I have to watch you die?

Angry and grief-stricken, I pretended all was fine. I showered in the morning, put on makeup, kissed the boys goodbye and then practically ran to the car to get out of that house.

Howard came into the newsroom around 4 p.m. one day, wearing khakis, loafers and a white sweater over button-down collar. Howard was the county editor. Together, we worked on my stories. I couldn't help but notice Howard's blue eyes behind his wire-rimmed glasses. They were the same color as my father's – robin's egg blue.

A standout he wasn't with his gray hair and deep creases leading from his mouth to his chin. I doubt if many women had found him irresistible, but his intelligence and his kindness touched me. And he was healthy.

There was no denying it. I had a crush on Howard. At least he was divorced. When I got into bed at night and fantasized about the two of us kissing and making love, I didn't feel guilty as I had with Father Todd. I knew it was escapism.

I lost myself in crafting words into something meaning-ful, sweeping my own sexual desires under the rug. Maybe more than Howard, the writing inspired my passion. My love of writing would see me through the loneliest and darkest days of my life.

Chapter Nineteen

It had been seven years since he'd first been diagnosed. There had been CT scans, bone scans, MRIs, radiation, ultrasounds and chemotherapy.

"What new test will medical science dream up?" John asked.

All of it merging now into one long, unforgiving illness. I'd get home and find my husband asleep on the couch, under an afghan. An old movie was running on the VCR.

"The worst time for me is after dark," he told me. "The house is quiet and I can't sleep."

All these years he had been terrified, horrified by what was happening to his body. I knew he viewed it as a personal failure; that he had let me down. Yet he kept it from me as he fought his solitary battle with cancer. His honor had been at stake. That battle he had surely won.

I had a flashback - him whispering how much he loved me. He made it so easy for the girl who had once felt unattractive. With him, I was lovely and desirable. With him, I became a wife and a mother. I became a woman.

As the cancer ate him bit by bit, John slowly disappeared, the vibrant man I loved now a haggard, foul-smelling scarecrow. He spent his days with Daniel, taking his child on errands, buying him every toy he wanted.

He had started writing about his battle with cancer. *"Most cancers don't fight a conventional war. Like the enemy in Vietnam during my war, it is fighting a war of attrition. He prefers to show himself only when he has the odds in his favor. He builds up his forces and stays hidden not showing any symptoms until he knows the odds are on his side."*

Still, I fought for him, for us, in my desperate attempts to defeat the enemy.

I spoke to a medical reporter at the paper about shark cartilage, which was being touted like the old black magic as a possible cure for cancer. She ended up researching it and turning it into a story. Although it didn't seem like a good bet, he tried it, along with organic produce. Soon, the juicer was stained orange by so many shredded and mashed carrots.

One night I woke with a start. John was rolling back and forth on the hallway floor, his knees scrunched up to his chest in terrible pain.

"I'll call 911." I ran into the bedroom and grabbed the phone.

About ten minutes later, the red ambulance lights flared in the driveway.

"Just go back to bed," he said, turning to look at me as they wheeled him out on a stretcher. "You need to be here for the boys."

It was 3 a.m. The silence and the tick of the clock on the mantle in the living room were my only companions. I curled up in bed clutching an old teddy bear.

Again in a Heartbeat

They inserted a stent to relieve fluid build-up from a blockage in his urethra. CT scans also showed a tumor on his lung.

We had rented a house in Ocean City, New Jersey, for a week in July. Suddenly, John had decided he wasn't going.

"I need you to go to the Shore with the boys and me!"

"I'm too sick!" John shouted.

"Then leave!" I screamed. "What good are you as a father if you can't even go with us on vacation? Some days I wish I'd never met you!"

I knew how horrible I sounded. I wanted to pull the words back inside of me, but it was too late. I couldn't breathe for a second. Just then I heard him grab the keys off the hall table, slam the front door, gun the car and drive off.

I paced in the living room. Suppose he never comes back? Maybe it would be for the best. He was sick. The last thing he needed now was a shrew just like his mother.

I drove to the convenience store and bought a pack of cigarettes even though I hadn't smoked in years. I inhaled, willing myself to push back the panic and shame.

He came home an hour later. It was a dismal, rainy day. He was wearing the long-sleeved brown corduroy shirt I had given him the previous Christmas, 1993.

"I'm sorry. I didn't mean what I said." The tears welled in my throat.

He looked at me. He took off his wedding ring and placed it on the table.

"You never deserved this." He went upstairs. I heard the door close to the study.

I followed him. I sat next to him on the faded white couch. The table next to us was covered with prescription drugs, including morphine. Each orange jar stood next to the other like a row of little soldiers lined up to fight the war. A war, even I knew now, we were losing.

"I didn't mean what I said. It's just that I can't bear to live without you."

He smiled. "You are more than you know, Susan. You will hurt. But you will survive."

He put his arm around me. "Best meal ever."

"Crab salad. Blue Moon Saloon, Redondo Beach, California," I automatically responded, playing our game.

"Seals sunbathing on the rocks," John smiled.

"We could see them from the windows of the restaurant," I finished.

At that I cried. For all that had been, for all that would never be. California. It was our dream. I touched his face. He had grown a beard and it was tinged with gray. My heart was breaking. He took my hand and pressed his lips into my palm. He wiped my tears away with his fingertips.

"We had a good ride," he said.

I felt bitterness well up in my throat like vomit. No, I wanted to shout. No. Don't leave me.

Chapter Twenty

John did the "thinking for the two of us," as Bogie would say.

The cancer had continued to invade and his kidneys shut down. The doctor explained that we were "one of the lucky ones" because we could rob the cancer of its worst ravages simply by John going off dialysis.

Watching my husband die did not make me feel like I was "one of the lucky ones."

"It's all working out for the best," he said.

"What do you mean?" I asked, dreading his answer.

"I want to go out on my own terms, not on some doctor's." He looked out the window. Alex and Daniel were playing touch football with their friends. "I don't want the boys to see some long-drawn-out death scene."

"The cancer," he said. He paused, considered. "I remember when I taught Chekhov. Cancer is like a character from one of his plays that has moved into our home and into our family and just sits in the dark corners. There's never any peace. Is this trip too much on John? Can John digest that kind of food? Oh, John's too tired to do that today. The whole scene has just been too much for the family."

He turned and looked at me. "Dialysis. I want to stop. Do you agree?"

The tuna fish sandwich I had eaten for lunch roiled around in my stomach. I couldn't find my voice. He felt responsible, guilty. I was healthy, the boys were healthy. He was alone in this.

He reached for my hand. "Susan."

I found my voice around the lump in my throat. "There has to be some way. I should have done more for you."

He smiled. "Susan, you have always been too hard on yourself. What could you do? I played the hand I was dealt. I have no regrets."

Would I in years to come replay this conversation, despising myself for feeling relief that it was finally coming to an end?

"You've suffered enough." The words caught in my throat.

He let out a sigh. "Good. It is settled."

"Come here," he smiled and looked deeply into my eyes. "I told Alex the other day; never question your mother. She is a very wise woman. In all the years I have known her she has never been wrong."

"You told him that?"

"It's true. Look at you. Tall, beautiful and strong. A reporter with *The Philadelphia Inquirer.*"

It was 1994, October, my favorite time of the year. The Halloween witch, with her broomstick and gnarly hands that he had given to me as a gift two years before, was slowly revolving on the hearth in the family room downstairs.

Again in a Heartbeat

The maple tree had turned a vivid crimson and orange. In years past, we would rake the leaves and stuff them into huge trash bags that looked like Halloween pumpkins with bulging jack-'o-lantern grins.

Brandy was barking at the next door neighbor. The front door slammed. The boys' footsteps pounded up the stairs. All I had ever wanted was this; to be with my husband and my children.

"At least you have a single house instead of a townhouse to raise the boys. It's not the greatest place, but it will do," he was saying.

John began jotting things down in his neat printing. "This is all our bank account and financial information, what you can expect to get from the company."

This is insane, making a smooth transition from his demise to my widowhood. Will someone please wake me up?

My fingers itched for the pack of cigarettes in my sweater pocket.

He saw my gesture. "Go ahead. It's not like the smoke can give me cancer," he joked.

He put the notepad aside and stood up. "I'm going to call Steve," he said referring to his oncologist.

I waited, inhaled deeply. I could hear the hum of something. Oh yes, the dishwasher. He came back into the den.

"Tomorrow," he said. "Steve says I can check into the hospital tomorrow."

The next day the sky was a pure flawless blue.

John looked out our bedroom window. "As the Indians would say, today is a good day to die."

Steve had agreed to let John discontinue dialysis and die at the hospital. John moved to the bed and sat down. "You're too smart for most men." He was putting on his socks and shoes as we got ready to drive to the hospital for the last time.

"You'll remarry. I will be jealous, but I want you to be happy," he went on as though he would be watching me in the afterlife.

I sat down on the bed next to him. "I don't want another husband. I want you," I cried.

"Believe me, I wish I had a choice," he said grimacing in pain. He touched his stomach. "I can feel it," he said as though the cancer were a living, breathing demon inside of him. "It is moving faster now."

"Just do me one favor," he said. "Don't let the boys call another man dad."

With that he stood up. He went toward the closet where his shirts and pants and dress suits hung neatly in a row. His West Point saber that Louise had used sixteen years ago to stab me through the hand rested against a wall in the closet.

He pulled out his old tan sweater. For a brief moment, he leaned his head against the closet door. Gone was his vow to beat the odds. In that moment, I saw his defeat. The enemy had won.

Daniel, who had turned seven years old on John's forty-seventh birthday the month before, ran into the bedroom, alleviating the horror of the moment.

"Daddy, Alex won't let me play with his Transformers," he cried in an outraged high-pitched voice.

"Come here," John said pulling his son to him. Daniel was wearing a red tee shirt with Darth Vader on the front.

"It's ok, Daniel," John said letting him go. "Your brother will let you share if you ask nicely."

Daniel ran back down the hallway to Alex's room, shouting, "Alex, Dad says you have to let me play with your toys."

How was I ever going to manage without my husband, the father of my children? My hands were ice cold. I was shivering as if it were January.

"What do you want me to do with your clothes?" I was feeling like it wasn't really me in the room, but someone playing a part. Someone directed me to stay steady. It was my strength now, not his, that kept me going.

"I saved some things. Give the rest away," John said.

He had neatly packed in boxes some of his old Army uniforms from West Point for sentimental reasons - shirts with his insignia and name tag; as orderly a leave-taking as if he were a soldier heading off for overseas duty. Only he wouldn't be returning.

I felt as though he was already gone. In some strange, dark part of me, I wanted it done so I could rest.

Yet would it have changed anything if I had known that he was going to get sick? I had taken the vows - "in sickness and in health" - not realizing how fraught with meaning they would be. I was naïve enough to believe we had years ahead of us that day we married at Wayne Presbyterian Church.

Now, we walked downstairs with a suitcase. John had packed his Bible and a framed picture of the boys and me. He stood in the foyer and checked his pants pockets for his wallet. He had lost so much weight his slacks hung like bags around his legs. His shoulder bones were protruding under his maroon plaid shirt. He took one last look around the living room.

"Well, this is it, I guess," he said. "I won't be coming back here again."

The babysitter, a fourteen-year-old girl with her ash blond hair pulled back into a ponytail, arrived. I opened the door and she looked at us brightly.

"Hi. How are you?"

What to say to this chirpy teenage girl? *Oh we're fine. I'm getting ready to drive my husband to the hospital where he should be dead in five days. Just remember if you are ever lucky enough to fall in love make each day count because you never know when it could all be over.*

Instead, I said, "There's apple juice and pizza for dinner. Don't let the boys argue you into staying up past ten."

"No problem," she smiled heading upstairs.

John and I got into the car. "Maybe there will be a miracle," I said.

"Maybe," John said.

We drove to the top of our street to make a right hand turn out onto the highway. As we waited for the traffic, he said, "I'm not going to miss this place."

It came as a startling revelation. For six years we had lived in an old-fashioned clapboard house on a cul-de-sac where the kids could play basketball in the summer and set up lemonade stands. Not an exciting place, but a good one to raise children. I thought we had been happy. He had never said otherwise.

Does anyone ever really know another person as well as they think, even when he is your best friend and husband? I wanted to believe I knew every part of John. Now I realized how foolish I had been.

The time for questioning was past. He had waged a battle against the disease. He was too tired to fight anymore. We were heading toward our final destination - or John was. My destiny had now become as murky as that foggy runway in *Casablanca.*

Chapter Twenty-One

John turned his final days into a party. His classmates from West Point traveled from Connecticut and Georgia, six-packs of Coors in hand, and reminisced about the good old days as cadets. John's hospital room resounded with raucous laughter about what an "asswipe" Company Commander So and So had been.

"Hey, that bastard wrote me up and gave me demerits because there was pubic hair in my soap dish," John joked.

"Come on, Cav, you were a rebel," his classmate, Jim, rejoined. "You never cared about a few demerits."

As the morphine and Coors eased John out of this life, they partied. I planned the funeral arrangements.

"Italians always have viewings. Make sure I'm wearing a red necktie. It's a good color on me," John said in all seriousness.

"Do you think it is a good idea for the boys to see you like *that?*"

He shrugged. "Keep them at home then. But I want a viewing."

I knew I would never look at him in a casket. It was ghoulish, uncalled for to ask that of me. It must have been his latent Catholicism coming through. But let him talk, I thought.

He wanted to be buried at West Point. He looked off in the distance, lost in a memory of when he was young and healthy, not as white as the hospital sheets that covered him.

"I remember those spring days, the Plain, a parade in full dress uniform." He stopped, smiled. "The huge crowds in short sleeves and sunglasses rimming the parade field. The band is playing the official West Point march or 'Army Blue.' Call me a sentimental fool. I want to be there."

Which suit to bury you in, my love, which necktie? I decided he should wear his wedding ring. His friends advised I not place his West Point ring in the coffin. Save it for the boys, they said. I simply nodded and did what they suggested. Having other people tell me what to do was a relief.

I took Alex and Daniel to the hospital one last time. John asked them how their soccer teams were doing, how school was going.

"Be good boys and take care of your mother," he said. He hugged them.

No death scenes had been his last wish. I think the boys thought it was just another hospital visit and he would be coming home. I felt so sorry for my sons. I had to make things right for them now and always. It helped keep me strong.

She was there when I visited him the last time. Her name was Casey. She was the wife of his West Point classmate.

"Hello, Susan," she said.

"Hello, Casey."

Short blond hair framed her cherubic face. I could hardly believe her nerve. She had *actually* shown up.

I had met her the month before. John and I had driven to Westport, Connecticut to visit Richard, her husband, and John's West Point classmate. Casey and Richard knew John was terminal.

Richard was an alcoholic. She was a devout Catholic.

Their son, Jason, had been born handicapped. Although he was eighteen years old, he had the intelligence of a four year old. I thought she was into social climbing and appearances. Her son and her husband's alcoholism were hampering her attempts to fit into Westport's elite hierarchy. Casey showed us a sample of brocade wallpaper. She had an interior design business and said it might look "perfect" in a dining room she was redoing for a "a very demanding" client up the street. The client was a well-known talk show host.

My husband was dying and she was going on about wallpaper and celebrities.

It was a lovely afternoon with a hint of fall in the air. A group of us, all married couples, sat on the deck. We ate crackers and crab dip while we sipped expensive wine.

John felt so ill he had gone into the house to lie down. I went to find him. I heard voices. I walked down the hallway where there was a small bedroom. That's when I saw Casey sitting by his side, holding his hand.

"It's okay, honey. You won't be alone," she said stroking John's dark hair. "I'm going to be right there with you when those angels come to take you to heaven. You're going to have a special place with them. I can see it now - the angels fussing all over you. Of that, I have no doubt!"

I stood in the shadows of the hallway. I watched my husband squeeze her hand. "You're an angel, Casey. Will you come to the hospital at the end?"

"Of course," she said.

At that moment, I hated her. I almost hated John. I felt betrayed. I had been there from the beginning, not her! How could he? I would be the widow, the odd man – or, in this case - woman out, raising his sons, trying to make ends meet. She would remain in her snobbish world, thriving next year on someone else's tragedy.

I went back out onto the deck.

Everyone was laughing and drinking. The sun was starting its descent behind towering trees, rays of gold slanting through their branches like arrows pointed straight at my heart. Another woman, one safer than I, was what he needed now and in whom he found solace. They came out later. I looked at John, so gaunt. We never spoke of what happened.

Now here she was, my husband's "angel" while I stood helpless and afraid on the fifth floor of the hospital. She made me feel like an intruder at the most private moment of my marriage.

She smiled when I stepped into the room. "A little while ago he told me he saw people in white robes coming for him. He is almost with God now."

Her smug religious claptrap reinforced my instinct that I had been right about her. But I said nothing. John's death deserved dignity. I just wanted her gone.

She stood up, smoothed her black skirt. "I'll leave you two alone," she said. With that, she walked out of his room. I never saw her again.

Death had entered the hospital room. I could not bear to see it hold him and take him. Had John known how terrified, how horrified I was of this final moment? Is this why he wanted Casey by his side, who when death pounced, welcomed it like an old friend?

I could see that John was deep inside a place, gone from me. I moved to his bedside.

"I will always love you." I kissed his forehead, held his hand. I studied his long beautiful fingers one last time, his hands that had once defined me.

"You are all I ever wanted," I whispered. "Sleep now, my love."

I left the room. It was the last time I ever looked at my husband's face.

Chapter Twenty-Two

It was minutes after midnight when the phone rang and the disembodied voice of some cancer ward nurse told me my husband had suffered "a bad night." After much tossing and turning, he "expired." They never said "died" or "dead."

I felt a curious numbness. I went downstairs to tell Alex. He had fallen asleep watching television on the couch, but woke up when the phone rang. Daniel was asleep upstairs in his room with his Transformers and stuffed animals.

I gave Alex the news that his father was now in heaven, freed from his suffering. Alex stared up at the ceiling for a moment. Without a word, he closed his eyes and went back to sleep.

I walked out on the deck. A full harvest moon hung in the October sky. I remembered the night John and I stood on the balcony at Mellon Hall under the same moon. That night I whispered in his ear that he was sexier than Paul McCartney.

"But not as rich," he had said.

What good were riches now? What good had riches ever been if he was not by my side?

I ran to the forsythia bushes and in fury began pulling at and breaking off the slender branches one after another. Spent, I fell to my knees and sobbed.

I went back into the house. Alex slept peacefully. I looked at a framed print of Andrew Wyeth's Helga I had hung in the family room where my son slept. She was wearing a long dark green cloak. One booted toe rested on a snow-covered boulder. Her back leaned against a gigantic oak trunk. Unlike Helga, I no longer had my oak tree. It had been felled.

PART TWO

Chapter Twenty-Three

Outside the window, dirty snow had given away to brown patches of grass. It was the winter of 1995 . . . John had been dead for three months.

I looked at Shirley through a blur of tears. "It's not fair. He was too young, too good a person. He didn't deserve what he got. I didn't deserve him."

"He loved you, Susan."

"I promised I wouldn't let anything happen to him. I couldn't keep my promise," I sobbed. Shirley specialized in grief counseling. I paid her sixty-five dollars an hour to cry in privacy.

"You were losing your dreams. You were losing your future," Shirley said. "You're too hard on yourself."

I smiled weakly. "John said that to me, too."

A week before I had been cleaning out John's dresser drawer when I found his notebook. *Cancer is a day-to-day emotional war. The relationship between me and my loving wife can never be the same. Like a husband who has admitted that he has a mistress, I don't think that my wife feels she can ever fully trust me again. I have betrayed her by allowing this beast to enter our lives. I have somehow managed to wreck our happy home and put all our futures in jeopardy. I, as a man, somehow feel that I am a failure. The disease has to be a weakness. The cancer has to be because of something that I did. I don't believe that and neither does my wife, but that's what cancer does to you – it plays with your mind and your values. It shows no mercy.*

Marathon phone conversations with Denise, my best friend and the sister I never had, helped save my life. I could tell her everything going back to when we were twelve and played with Barbie and Ken dolls at the picnic table in her leafy backyard.

"I shouldn't have yelled at him toward the end," I said.

"You had two kids to raise, a job," Denise said. "You have to forgive yourself. John knew that you loved him. And he adored you."

There was a hard lesson. Forgiving myself because I was certain that other women in the same situation would have been kinder, would have been smarter . . . would have saved him and us.

Shirley said it might help if I talked to another widow. Lorraine phoned me one night. I told Lorraine I felt like I was going crazy. She said the feeling of going crazy was normal – she felt it too after her husband died and that the first three to six months were the hardest. After that it would get better.

Lorraine suggested a support group. I drove to Media and found the family therapy building next to a Methodist church. About a dozen women and one man stood in a row with folding chairs arranged in a circle.

I stuffed my hands deeper into the pockets of my long, gray winter coat. This place had no bearing to my life. My life was with John and the boys. In my mind, I was still John's wife.

Everyone was older than I, so old I felt I had stumbled into a gathering of my parents' friends. That's when I realized just how young I was to be widowed.

Meryl, the therapist running the group, approached me.

"Welcome, Susan," she said. She was close to six feet tall, wore a black dress and matching pumps. Her hair looked like spun yellow cotton candy. She asked me how old John was when he died.

"I'm sorry," she said with a practiced tone of condolence after I told her. "My first husband died at the age of thirty-nine after dropping dead on the basketball court of a massive heart attack. I spent twenty-five years as a single woman before I met my second husband. He's a wonderful man."

I suppose she felt she was offering hope. After a quarter of a century, I, too, might again find a husband.

One at a time we went around the circle, introducing ourselves. A woman named Betsy went first. Her husband died of pancreatic cancer.

"He was gone in twelve days after the diagnosis," she said. She adjusted her glasses. "That was six months ago. It's time to move on."

Betsy was overweight and in her early sixties. She wore silver peace sign earrings. Her painted fingernails were shiny maroon.

She posted her profile on an Internet dating site. She drove miles to a café in Manayunk to meet a man. All that

> never showed. She was filled with bravado
> ory.

> hat he stood me up. When I got home, I sent
> .. angry email. I know I'm wonderful so I don't let it
get to me." She held up her handbag. It was cherry red and
decorated with a big rhinestone peace symbol.

"I saw this in one of the shops in Manayunk that day and
bought it, along with these," she said touching her earrings.
"I thought I would treat myself."

"Good for you," Meryl said. "It's important that we
pamper ourselves. Don't give up on the dating," she advised.

The lone man, who looked to be in his late sixties, wore
a business suit.

"Hi. My name is Harry. My wife, Bernice, died of
Alzheimer's."

Harry said that in the months before his wife lost her
memory, he pasted post-it notes to kitchen cabinets and
drawers so she could remember where she kept the spoons,
the plates.

"I can barely scramble an egg. And I hate eating alone,"
he said.

I looked around the circle. The women leaned forward
in their chairs. Heads nodded in sympathy.

When it was my turn, I found myself talking as if it were
someone other than me. There was no emotion in my voice,
just me pretending I wasn't as angry as I felt. I said I was a
reporter, had two sons. What I wanted to say was I wondered
how I could ever have a decent life without John. And that
the one person I wanted to talk to about all of this was him.

Afterwards, Meryl suggested that we exchange phone
numbers and emails, if we wanted. "It is important to support
each other. There are singles group all around the area. It

is fun to get out, even if it is just to grab a bite to eat or meet someone new."

What could possibly be fun about being single, I wanted to shout. I'm too old for dating! I have two children, for god's sake.

Over coffee and cake, the women congregated and fluttered around Harry. I grabbed my coat and quietly slipped out the front door.

That week I signed up for a tai chi class. "Say hello to feeling cool, calm, and energized," the adult night school brochure advertised. I figured it beat sitting in a circle of depressed women looking for husbands.

Chapter Twenty-Four

Over the next several months, work helped me focus. One day I scored a front page story about a second grade teacher who had used the only two African American students in her class to stage a mock slave auction. The story was picked up by the Associated Press and the Phil Donahue Show.

At home, I helped the boys with homework. I cooked dinner. I thought about the man at the support group who wanted a wife to cook for him. There would be no wife for me. I kept a journal in the top drawer of my night table. After the boys went to bed, I started writing as Brandy lay curled at my feet. *This spring the forsythia bloomed so bright and so briefly . . . like his time with me, it was gone in a heartbeat.*

I stopped going to see Shirley. There was no solution to grief. It just tunneled inside you, getting uglier and uglier. She couldn't bring John back. And all that talk of how he loved me made it worse.

Me shouting at him in the kitchen that day, "I wish I'd never met you!"

Sometimes, I danced with John again in my dreams. I felt the warmth of his body; saw the look in his eyes as he slowly began making love to me.

"I've put you through enough these last seven years," he said.

"Please don't go," I begged. But he left anyway, disappearing up a winding staircase. I would wake up in my bedroom with the same flowered wallpaper that had been there when he was alive, only now the room was laden with the heavy fragrance of grief.

California, dancing at our sons' weddings, growing old together . . . all shattered on October 12, 1994, the day he died.

Financially, I was not as bad off as many widows. I had John's life insurance and double his salary – not a lot, but a decent amount. That, plus my salary, Social Security survivors' benefits for Alex and Daniel and VA benefits, kept us comfortable.

At night I watched the recap on television of the OJ Simpson trial. Outside, the silvery moon cast light behind clouds scuttling across the sky. John and I had been good people. We hadn't hurt anyone. My dream of happily-ever-after mocked me.

Some days, I found myself crying over stupid things, like the fragile beauty of a bright red cardinal perched on the forsythia branch.

That May – seven months after John died - my father suffered a cerebral hemorrhage. By the time the ambulance arrived at Paoli Memorial Hospital, he was gone. My mother, who depended on him for everything, collapsed. She once

told me, "I'm afraid of life. I always have be⸍
up to me to protect and care for my mothⲅ
I could do. Although she had been critiⲥ⸍
often too outspoken and not as feminine as a girⳑ ⸍
I never came home without dinner on the table and ⲦⲮ
artfully arranged in ceramic vases throughout the house. She
did the best she could, considering her nervous and fragile
disposition.

I became her power-of-attorney. My brother, Andy, a
successful businessman, left her caretaking to me. I cleaned
out and sold my parents' twin home in Exton, keeping for
myself my grandmother's antique French marble mantle
clock and twelve crystal stemware goblets from Germany.
Then I moved Mother to an assisted living community in
West Chester where her anxiety and the beginning of
dementia could best be treated. I could visit her as often as
I liked.

In late September, 1995, I drove up along the Hudson
River to West Point. Alex didn't want to come, so I took
Daniel. The wind kicked up. There was a bite coming off the
Hudson.

I laid one long-stem yellow rose at the foot of the little
white granite tombstone. I remembered John's laughter as
we stood under Kissing Rock the first year we were married.
"Come here, Mrs. Cavalieri. Let me kiss you." I needed to
believe we surrendered our hearts for a reason. Otherwise, if
we knew how it was going to end, who would chose this pain?

"Why did Dad want to be buried here?" Daniel asked.

I put my arm around his thin shoulders. "Your dad was
very proud of being a West Point graduate. In some ways, it
defined his dreams before you and Alex and I came into his
life."

"Do you think I should come here when I grow up, Mom?"

I swallowed hard. "If that's what you want. But remember. Your dad is already proud of you. I know he can see us and is watching us now."

I wanted to believe that. I suppose it gave me solace.

Daniel and I walked from the cemetery to the car. The echoes of cadets' voices drifted from the Plain above. John belonged here. Like a good soldier he had fought for seven years. Now an honorable man had been laid to rest. My life was back in Chester Springs with our sons.

Chapter Twenty-Five

I was forty-five years old. Not old, not young. Move on with your life, friends told me. I wanted to scream.

I ran into Marcia in January, 1996. We had known each other as neighbors when John and I lived in Frazer. She had heard about John and his long illness and offered her sympathy.

Her long brown hair was held back with a headband, but the girlish look was offset by her deeply lined face, the product of chain smoking and too many hours in the tanning salon. She divorced her husband, Joe, after he charged thousands of dollars in credit card debt to buy his twenty-something girlfriend presents.

"I found her business card in his suitcase," she said flatly.

Since the divorce, Marcia had been seeing a married man. As soon as he got it together, he was going to leave his wife, she insisted.

"His wife is busting his balls," Marcia said.

I let Marcia drag me to a nightclub in Radnor. Men with pot bellies and women with cleavage gyrated across the dance floor. A disco ball splintered red and gold light across the excess flab and flesh. Isn't this fun? *Smile,* Marcia told me.

When Matthew, her married man, showed up, he drank too many beers, smoked too many cigarettes and barely acknowledged me. He grabbed Marcia by the arm and led her out to the dance floor. The noise, the smoke, the desperation drove me outside where I took in big gulps of frigid night air. I found my car in the jammed parking lot and sped back to safety. Back to my bedroom, back to the little journal where I poured out grief.

Why me? What did John and I do to deserve this? None of it makes sense. I see people who smoke and drink themselves into oblivion. They are walking around, healthy and happy.

On weekends, Alex and Daniel huddled over video games with friends. I cooked French toast and bacon, shuttled the boys to the mall or the movies. It was good to hear the laughter and voices of children in the house. The boys didn't ask a lot about their father, but I often talked about John to them.

I was lonely. My father and husband were dead. My mother was in a retirement home, living on pills and antidepressants. John's family had abandoned us. Big Mike had died of a heart attack in 1992. Louise and John's brother, Michael, wanted nothing to do with us. Our relationship had never recovered after the saber-stabbing incident.

Ross, a neighbor whose daughters were friends with my boys, started dropping by. One day he helped me put the shower rod back up. It had fallen with a loud bang. I was so grateful I must have thanked him twenty times. A little later, I heard a knock. He handed me a CD of songs he had written and recorded.

"Maybe it could get a mention in the community arts column of the *Inquirer*?" he suggested.

He was wearing a black pullover sweater, faded blue jeans and sneakers. He sat down on the flowered sofa in my living room. Could he impose for a cup of coffee?

His company wanted to transfer him to Michigan. It was a promotion, but he turned it down and then quit. "I want custody of my girls so I have to stay here," he said.

Since his wife had filed for divorce, his plan was to start his own consulting business. The cut in income would serve his wife right, he said. I had met his wife, Nan, once. Their daughter, Amanda, and Daniel were in the same grade.

"Nan's not working?" I asked, handing him a steaming mug of coffee.

Ross snorted and shook his head. He leaned toward me. A dimple creased his cheek when he smiled.

"I admire you. A single mother working full time after what you've been through. And a reporter with the *Inquirer*. Wow. Very impressive."

I looked away from his hazel eyes. It had been a while since a man had shown interest in me.

"I'm lucky. I love my job." He sat so close I could smell his soap and aftershave.

"But what about you? How are you doing?" I heard the nervousness in my voice.

"I was a lousy husband, according to her. A lousy husband." His voice dripped with scorn.

"I bought her a house with a swimming pool. She could sit home all day and do whatever she wanted. Now she wants fifty-five percent of my assets."

Trashing his wife sounded immature.

117

He told me he slept in the master bedroom. Nan moved into the guest room. "My lawyer says I'll lose the house and my daughters if I move out. My wife and her high-powered attorney, paid for by her mother I might add, could get me on abandonment."

He stood up. "A divorce is nothing compared to what you've been through. I'm sorry I never got a chance to meet John."

He touched my arm. "Thanks for the coffee."

Flustered, I nodded. His self-centeredness had given away to kindness.

After he left, I found myself thinking about him. He was good-looking. Was he using me for free publicity?

I went into the kitchen and brewed another pot of coffee. Some days I felt like a victim of post traumatic stress disorder, always on the alert for the next disaster. I felt I had to be constantly vigilant or my family could end up ruined. The news media wrote about the trouble boys without fathers got into. I wished I had someone. I wished my sons had a father.

I called Denise. "Do you think it's too soon to start dating again?"

"Of course not. John would want you to be happy."

"What about you?" I asked. "Are you seeing anyone?"

She laughed. "I don't have time, I'm so busy working."

Denise worked as a reporter for a weekly newspaper in New Jersey. Unlike the *Inquirer*, there was no union. She was overworked and underpaid.

Denise married her first husband right out of college. "He was more interested in chess tournaments than me," she said. Her second husband refused to have children. After that, she hooked up with a divorced man. He left for a woman practicing witchcraft he met on the Internet.

"Men are just too much work," Denise sighed, as we spoke on the phone into the late hours of the night. "They put you on a shelf, dust you off and take you down when they want. Then they put you back on the shelf. It's probably why I've put on so much weight. I took myself out of the game. You were lucky to have John."

I knew what she meant. Most men were not John.

Chapter Twenty-Six

July arrived with long, languid, days. I had been born in July. My father planted a rose of sharon bush in the backyard when I was a little girl. Its vivid purple and pink blossoms opened on July 11, my birthday. After that, Dad called it "Susie's rose of sharon."

I missed my father. I missed watching him in the old tan chair in the living room work a crossword puzzle, a copy of his favorite novel, *Moby Dick*, on the table beside him. I missed the sound of my mother in the kitchen, making fresh rhubarb stew and ice tea garnished with spearmint from our garden.

I remembered how the hummingbirds were drawn to the rose of sharon blossoms. In those days and months after John and my father died, the longing and feelings of loss left me as unprotected as a thirsty hummingbird drawn by the promise of sweet, ripe nectar.

"What are you doing?"

My heart beat faster as I held the phone. "I was paging through summer camp catalogues for the boys. I need a break from parenting."

"Good idea. Nan and the girls are gone for the weekend. I would love to see you. Do you want to come over for a glass of wine?"

Ross's invitation took me by surprise. Or maybe I was out of practice. I hadn't dated in almost twenty years. It was exactly eight o'clock and I was already in pajamas.

"Okay," I said.

I threw on a pair of jeans and my black John Lennon tee shirt with *Imagine* in white letters. Then I walked a few blocks past manicured lawns, up the hill and across the street to his neighborhood of McMansions. The huge brick and stone houses loomed ghostly in the night, the silence of suburbia punctuated by the distant barking of a dog.

I knocked on the massive oak door. He greeted me with a guitar slung over his shoulder. "I want to play my new song for you," he announced.

A large, framed poster of Bob Dylan hung in the high ceiling foyer. It was like Dylan was staring right at me. Outside the family room window, steam rose from a hot tub's aquamarine depths. I wondered how the steamy water would feel against my skin. When was the last time I had given myself permission to have fun?

"So what do you think?"

"Excuse me?"

"My song? Did you like it?"

I lied. "It was good. Very good."

"Thanks," he said leaning the guitar up against the chair.

I watched as he stood up and put on an album. It was 1996 and he was still into vinyl. He had a casual grace like a panther as he moved toward the record player. He chose a Tim Buckley album. The songs were a haunting reminder of college when everything seemed possible.

"It's beautiful music." I could finally say that honestly.

His hand lightly touched my arm then moved away. "I'm glad you came tonight."

Ross's thigh pressed against mine as he leaned forward and poured more wine into our glasses. He held his Pinot Noir to the light; swirled and smelled it before taking a sip. There was a confidence about him that bordered on smugness. He told me his divorce boiled down to a midlife crisis on the part of his wife whom he described as "illogical and irresponsible."

He grew up in Boston, one of six children. He avoided bullies who laughed at his first name, which was Salvatore. His middle name was Ross.

"You didn't want to grow up in an all-Irish neighborhood in Boston with a name like Salvatore," he said, no humor.

I told him how difficult it had been for John as an Italian American at West Point in 1970. Very few names ended in vowels and John had been ridiculed by an upperclassman named Felix Newton for using his spoon to eat spaghetti. Newton instructed John to cut his spaghetti with a fork and knife.

I remembered John saying, "Who was I, a Cavalieri, a second generation Italian-American, to argue with Cadet Felix Newton, a New England WASP, over how to eat spaghetti?"

The way John told the story was funny.

I wanted to talk more about John, but stopped . . .it seemed less than romantic.

Ross looked outside the window. "I should have told you to bring your suit. We could have sat in the hot tub."

"The hot tub would have been nice," I murmured.

He leaned closer. The heat of his body merged into mine as he started kissing me, slow, smooth and sensual.

My cheeks flushed. I pulled away.

"You're still living with your wife."

"But it's been so long for both of us," he said.

I grabbed my purse. "I should go."

He didn't protest.

That night, I lay awake. I got out of bed and checked my computer for an email from him. Should I send him a message? For an hour I played Solitaire, every few minutes going back to check my email. I had become as neurotic as my mother, pacing in front of the living room window watching for my father.

Ross called two days later.

"You were right to bail out the other night."

A rush of emotions swept through me - a combination of happiness and injured feelings.

"I have the feeling you want a commitment," he said. "And I just can't give you that."

I searched my mind. Had I appeared too serious? I remembered that night in Montreal when I accused John of being too serious. Now the shoe was on the other foot.

Chapter Twenty-Seven

A group of women sat in a circle in an enclosed sun porch. It was sunset and elongated rays of gold cast opaque dusty shafts across the floor.

The palm reader hardly looked the part - no heavy silver bracelets, hoop earrings or long gray hair. She wore a pink blouse, jeans and Nikes.

When she got to me, she studied my hand, traced the deeply imbedded lines of my palm with her forefinger. After a moment, she announced to the group, "Susan has two life-lines. She has lived a harder life than anyone in this room."

I felt grateful for this unexpected acknowledgment of my ordeal. I was into my second life . . . life after John. I rarely talked about John, except to Denise. People had accused me of putting John on a pedestal just because he *was* dead. I felt embarrassed to admit how much I missed him, so I said nothing. They didn't want to hear it. Grief and widowhood made a person stick out like a leper. Married women especially were often repelled and avoided me. They were afraid this could happen to them.

The truth was that being a single parent was hard. I had to be mother and father, nurturer and disciplinarian. The weekend before the palm reading, Daniel screamed at me. "I don't want to go to some stupid camp. You can't make me!" He ran out of the kitchen and slammed the front door behind him. Nevertheless, I continued folding socks, underwear and tee shirts, packing my sons' duffle bags for summer camp. I needed the time alone. Someday the boys would understand.

The day arrived to leave for camp. Daniel resisted right up to the last moment until Alex and I got in the car. Reluctantly, he climbed into the car holding his Gameboy. Then we made the five-hour drive west toward Pittsburgh.

After I dropped them off in the pine-scented woods of Ligonier, loneliness engulfed me. Like the cancer, it had always been there, waiting in the shadows.

Online dating sites were gaining traction. If nothing else, I could write about my experience. It was as good an excuse as any to experiment with this new way of meeting people in middle age. I went upstairs, flipped on the computer and trolled a popular Internet dating site.

One profile was entitled: "Captain Seeks First Mate." *Most important is the desire to begin over and put previous disappointments behind.*

Too depressed and angry, I thought scanning more profiles. I came to a photograph of a man who resembled an overweight Sean Connery. *I don't want to waste time with emails or phone conversations. The only way to tell if there is chemistry is to meet in person.* I wrote him a brief response. Before I could reconsider, I hit send.

Two days later, we met at an historic inn located in what was left of Chester County horse country. Fox hunting scenes hung on the dark green walls. I recognized Mack from his Internet photograph. The "few extra pounds" he had listed on his profile were apparent by the stretch of black shirt across his stomach.

He stood up and pulled out a barstool. Then, he motioned for the bartender. "Pick your poison," he said to me.

After I ordered a glass of Pinot Grigio, Mack grimaced as he moved his left leg, tightly encased in black Levis. He saw my look of concern.

"I tore my quadriceps, which is the largest muscle in the thigh, playing volleyball on a cruise ship."

His knee pressed against mine. I waited for a moment, and then discreetly moved away. Didn't he even have the courtesy to try and get to know me first?

It was strange, meeting people based on a photograph and brief description, almost like a job interview. I had regressed to blind dates. Only I wasn't dancing the box step in Mellon Hall with a cadet from Valley Forge Military Academy. I was in a bar with a divorced man trolling for sex.

"So. You're an airline pilot," I straightened up . . . tried to look interested. I was referring to Mack's "Lets Fly Together" profile. "That must be an interesting job. Where do you fly?"

"Mostly, Philadelphia to Dublin."

He saw the look on my face. "Don't be impressed. It's a blue collar job with white collar benefits."

Silence. I sipped my wine. "Have you been divorced long?" I asked.

"A year. My wife was a model. Gorgeous woman. I don't mean to sound shallow, but after a woman like her it's hard not to go for good looks. She was my second wife," he added, as though this explained things.

Mack told me they spent their honeymoon in Atlantic City. He named the hotel, an old art deco place on the boardwalk Dad had taken me to once. They were up in their room when she told him she had to head to the lobby to pick up a spare key. When she returned, she smelled of cigarette smoke.

The tip of Mack's jacket collar was up on one side next to his mouth. It looked like one of those little microphones pilots speak into.

"I asked her if she had been smoking. She denied it," he said with derision. "I knew she was lying. Here I had married the woman and had no idea she was a smoker. Frankly, I never felt the same way about her again."

It reminded him of his mother, he added. "I always knew when she had been drinking because her mouth would go down on one side. But when I asked her, she said she hadn't had a drink."

Since lying had come up, I asked Mack how he knew whether people on the Internet were telling the truth.

Mack laughed. "I've met women who shave ten years off their age with old photos."

He pondered the stupidity of this as he drank his wine. When they met in the flesh, there was no resemblance. Not only were they fat; they were old.

I couldn't resist. "I should ask for your credentials. Are you really an airline pilot?"

Mack gave me a long, withering look through his gray-tinted glasses. He put his arm behind him to grab his wallet out of his back pants pocket. His black shirt stretched across his portly belly. John always had a firm stomach. And my husband never criticized me when I smoked.

"Here." Mack showed me a small card with tiny printing. Unless I fished my glasses from the bottom of my purse, there was no way I could read it.

I nodded. "So you are," I said to ease the tension.

Mack looked me up and down. "I noticed when I touched your knee, you pulled away."

"Well, I just met you," I said defensively. Oh, Jesus. There was no way I wanted to see this man naked. I wasn't ready for casual sex. Apparently, he was.

He shrugged. He looked around the bar. Two blonds sat in a corner.

I pulled out my purse. "Here's some money for my wine."

He didn't urge me to stay.

"I think I'll have another drink before I head out," he said.

As I drove from the inn to my house, I felt like a voyager leaving an emotional wasteland. Being a widow put me in a different "club" from divorced people. I had a hard time relating to stories of waking up to a stranger. Mack reminded me of an armadillo with his hardened shell. I pressed on the accelerator to get home faster.

If anything, John and I had been too close, too dependent on each other. We spent three nights apart when Unisys sent him to California on a business trip. Three nights out of seventeen years, except for his hospital stays.

I wasn't young anymore. In order for an older man to give up his independence after a divorce, a woman had to be everything *he* wanted. How could I adjust to this new life? And why would I want to?

Chapter Twenty-Eight

I hadn't been sleeping well. The world seemed to move around me, but I wasn't really a part of it anymore. I was on autopilot, taking care of the boys, stuck at the paper's suburban news bureau since I couldn't manage raising two children *and* working downtown where the real action lay. Motherhood was an occupational hazard, especially without a husband to help carry the load.

My best days were behind me. I felt sorry for myself. No one helped me with anything.

I went on another Internet date with Phil, who at fifty-eight, was twelve years older than I. My friends had suggested a widower instead of a divorced man. He'll have less baggage, they offered.

I walked into the West Chester restaurant and took off my sunglasses. Phil had snow-white hair and wore a navy blue wool sweater even though it was August. He looked to be about five feet, seven inches tall. On his Internet profile he listed himself as three inches taller. I was learning that women shaved off the pounds; men added the inches.

He was so worn down looking. His wife died of a stroke. The fact that we had experienced the same thing almost made him feel like family.

"So? You're a writer," Phil said. "What kind of writing?

"Newspapers."

"Are you going to write about this? The Internet?"

"I don't know. Maybe."

"It's okay. Just do me a favor. Don't use my real name." He grinned slyly, his hairy hand inching toward mine. I caught a whiff of mothball from his sweater.

Flirtation was beyond me. Even when I was young, I had never mastered it, nor wanted to. Now here I was with an old man. Although I was in my mid-forties, I still thought of myself as young.

I put my hands in my lap.

Phil's hand retreated. "I'm leaving soon. Getting out of Dodge. Taxes here are too high. Dreary winters, too."

The waiter brought our lunches.

"Where are you going?"

"New Mexico." Phil cut into his cheese omelet with a fork. "I'm buying a trailer home. Moving on."

I remembered Betsy, the widow at the support group. She used the same expression – *moving on.*

"Do think that's possible?" I asked. "Starting over at our age, I mean."

Phil put down his fork and reached for a paper napkin. "You got a pen?"

Puzzled, I reached into my purse and handed him one.

He drew a pyramid on the napkin. Then he drew a straight line across the bottom of the pyramid. "This group represents all the people married, in arrangements or whatever." He drew another line. "These are the people with alcohol and drug addictions." Another line up, he penned in a big, black letter N. "That's for all your nuts, your crazies."

All that was left of the pyramid was a tiny top tier; this represented possible partners.

"You see?" Phil smiled. "The odds aren't good."

This man depressed me, but I smiled.

After lunch we stood outside saying goodbye. "If you ever feel a need for your boot heels to be wandering, let me know. You have my email address," he said.

I walked along the sidewalk toward DeStarr's a Greek restaurant on Gay Street. I remembered the night John and I ate there. It was January, 1983. The snow drifted like huge, white marshmallows gleaming in the lamplight. When my stuffed grape leaves arrived, I felt ill. I was pregnant. I told John we were going to be parents.

He got up and walked around the table. Then he kissed me in front of the other diners. "I love you," he whispered into my ear. Outside, the wind blew the snow in swirls against the restaurant windows. Inside, I felt warm and full of life.

We came back to DeStarr's four years later after Daniel was born. It was a hot September day in 1987 with cornflower blue skies. So much had changed since I had been pregnant with Alex; John's diagnosis and cancer surgery - the fact that we couldn't have more children. The wolf was lurking at our door.

We drank big glasses of iced tea and ate gyros dripping with tzatziki sauce. Daniel was a week old and lay sleeping in his plastic carrier, his hand screwed up next to his ear, sucking on his binky. John and I held hands across the table. It was unimaginable that the cancer would rob him of watching his sons grow up. Even more unimaginable was that less than ten years later I would be meeting strange men for drinks and lunch.

Chapter Twenty-Nine

The summer of 1996 had stretched into fall. Charles, Prince of Wales and Diana had just divorced. The fairy tale romance had come to a crashing end.

I had a couple other dates through Match.com. I was discovering there were a lot of men on the Internet. If I wanted, I could have a date every weekend.

Ed was an engineer. People were jogging and walking their dogs as we sat on a park bench near a trail along the Brandywine Creek, a sparkling band of water that wove between banks of boulders and overhanging trees.

I was apprehensive that Ed might break down in tears as he told me his story. Ed had been his wife's caregiver, changing her bed sheets and monitoring her morphine after a long battle with breast cancer. She had pleaded to die. He finally complied and gave her an overdose. Although his wife had been dead for less than four months, he wanted to remarry. The quicker, the better. I felt as if her ghost were sitting between us.

A week later, I had another date.

"I've never been in love," Frank announced over lunch in Chestnut Hill, a charming town with tree-lined, cobble-stoned streets.

Even if it were true that he had never been in love, I would have been embarrassed to make that admission.

He was balding with a ponytail and his plaid cotton shirt was in need of ironing, a telltale sign of bachelorhood. Frank had married his wife out of obligation. They had been having sex for two years and she hinted she might "go off the deep end" if he didn't propose. Now they had two children and were divorced. Frank smoked marijuana to relax.

I munched on a chicken salad on white toast, trying to look sympathetic.

Outside it was a crisp fall day. The sunlight was a marvel of late September, gold and pure. The blue sky with streaks of white cloud seemed impossibly beautiful. I could be home reading a book, I thought, or walking my dog.

I wanted to like them, but their stories left me perplexed. How could you marry someone you didn't love? Ed couldn't even talk about his dead wife without tearing up, but was chomping at the bit to find a replacement. Anyone would do.

Then there was me. I had to wonder if the lonely, broken widow believed the only Prince Charming she would ever know was gone and she had to make do with this.

After those dates, I gravitated toward Ross. As his fingers worked expertly over the frets of his guitar and he hummed his new songs, I almost felt youthful and hopeful. Ross presented himself as a family man and, like John, he was Italian. Our children were friends. We clinked glasses of Shiraz and toasted to a brighter future. There was a sense of something happening, something new in the air. Or so I wanted to believe. There was no denying it. Sexual attraction was an aphrodisiac for grief.

Chapter Thirty

It was a Friday morning when Ross called to tell me he had signed the divorce papers. I knew what he wanted. He often said he couldn't commit until the divorce was final. Commitment was code for a sexual relationship while holding out the promise there might be more.

A few minutes later, Ross's green Dodge Caravan pulled into my driveway. I opened the front door. The cold of his nylon ski jacket pressed against my body as he hugged me. Neither of us spoke.

We made our way up the stairs to my bedroom. He pulled my sweater over my head, unhooked my bra with expert fingers. I unzipped his black Levis. He knew where to touch me.

Afterwards, I turned to look at him. He had a beautiful profile, a straight nose, firm chin. His chest hairs were a silvery gray like the hair on his head.

I had just made love to another man in the bed where John and I had conceived our sons. Strange, I thought. You wake up one day and find yourself confronted with a new reality that has nothing to do with your former life. You go on. What other choice is there.

Ross turned, startling me out of my reverie. "I'll bet you're happy I'm divorced."

"I think I may be falling in love with you," I whispered.

He stiffened like a man about to receive a shot of novocaine. "Don't make me say that word."

My cheeks flushed with humiliation. I got up to use the bathroom. I took a deep breath, drank a cup of water to quell the sickness in my stomach. When I came back into the bedroom, he was pulling on his jeans.

"I have to get going." His lips pecked my cheek. "You were great." He bounded down the stairs. I heard the front door close behind him.

I made a pot of coffee; drank one mug after another. The old feelings of insecurity kicked in.

That night Ross came over to my house. He was almost hurting me, he had me pressed so hard against the wall.

"So you love me?"

"You are the first man since my husband."

"I knew that. You know, I do love you."

I studied his face. "One minute you can't say or hear the words, the next you tell me you love me."

"You're smart. You're ambitious."

"What does that have to do with love?"

"Everything. Love is cerebral."

I wanted to argue that love was of the heart, but it seemed his mind was made up.

Later that night, Ross and I went to his house. His girls were with his ex-wife. I brought a bottle of champagne to celebrate his divorce. An eerie silence surrounded us. We sat at the kitchen table. The hood light from the stove cast a feeble glow in the darkness.

"My daughters mean everything to me," he said. "Nan won't destroy that."

Together, like two wounded animals, we walked upstairs. He lit vanilla-scented candles. Slowly, we peeled away each other's clothes. We lay down on the bed. His slightest move answered my cravings. We made love again and then again. Nan's pink curtains still hung at the bedroom windows that looked out on the dark cul-de-sac below.

Chapter Thirty-One

We sank into the hot tub.

"I'll bet I can find your G-spot," he said. His hand explored my bathing suit under the water. Ross was wearing skinny black nylon swim trunks that left nothing to the imagination. I always hated those. On him they looked good. Pinpricks of starlight studded a night sky so clear I could see the Big Dipper.

After I got home, Alex confronted me.

"You're not going to marry this guy are you?"

"Alex..."

"You are, aren't you?" he accused without letting me finish. "Did you know he set his ex-wife's chair on fire on the Fourth of July?"

I just looked at him. For a moment, I felt like laughing. This couldn't be true.

"Alex. . ."

"It's true, Mom. Gaby told me her dad was so angry he threw the chair in the backyard and set it on fire. Wake up! The guy's a control freak."

My son turned and walked out of the house. Was nothing easy? Couldn't my sons want the best for me? It was obvious Alex was not ready to see his father replaced. Daniel idolized his older brother and went along with whatever Alex said.

I wanted marriage again because I had a good marriage. People asked, why try to replace what had been that good? But no one wants to be alone.

Yet I knew there had been no soul-searching on my part. After John died, I took two weeks off from interviews and deadlines. I never retreated and mulled the meaning of my husband's death or the psychological impact of being single. I had run from the hopelessness of my situation and the tragedy of John's death.

I went upstairs to my bedroom and opened the closet door. I took the box off the shelf and lifted the lid. Inside were brightly colored neckties. I stroked the navy one with tiny white dots John had worn to the office. When would it be time to put this box away? I had no answer.

Chapter Thirty-Two

Christmas, 1996, was nearing. A real Scotch pine decorated with bubble lights stood next to the stone hearth in a corner of the restaurant. I had just finished interviewing a developer of corporate office parks. After he left, I ordered a Cosmopolitan.

I looked at the tree with the bubbles shooting up and down in red, green and purple. Bubble lights had been John's favorite ornaments and he insisted on buying them one Christmas. I hated those lights. We hung them on the tree, but they looked lopsided and clunky and ruined the symmetry of what I was trying to create . . . an elegant theme of gold and silver ornaments with tiny white lights. John bowed to my interior decorating edicts and his bubble lights got stashed among the cartons in the basement with the boys' old toys.

Appearances were destroying me. Society told me I needed a husband, to be part of a couple. I bought into it.

Did I really love Ross, I wondered as I paid for my drink? While he held out the promise of the big family I desired, he wanted things his way. Like not making love until the divorce was final. And never staying the whole night because he said it set a bad example for our children. He wasn't interested in my opinion.

And he was cheap. We had gone to an Indian restaurant because he had a coupon. He wanted me to pay half even though the night before I had been up to my wrists in Shake 'N Bake making fried chicken for his kids and mine. It all stemmed back to his anger over the divorce, being "taken to the cleaners," as he put it, by his ex-wife.

What a difference from my life with John! The gifts he had given me, the support and encouragement. John didn't complain when I took the job at the *Inquirer*, which paid less than Unisys. He knew I needed meaningful, creative work. Money didn't matter as long as I was happy.

The wine glasses I had bought Ross for Christmas were shoved to the back of my closet. I had waited to wrap them, hoping he might surprise me with a gift first. He hadn't.

I never worried much about finding someone to date when I was in my twenties. If it didn't work out with one guy, there was always another to take his place. Now that I was in my forties, that wasn't so easy. I saw the dwindling possibilities. "All the good ones are married" was a standing joke among my single friends. I thought of the pyramid Phil had drawn on the napkin. By the time you subtracted all the nuts and crazies, the pickings were slim.

I left the restaurant and felt a blast of damp, December air. It was hardly the season of cheer in our house. Alex self-medicated his pain. I found the beer cans behind a trash can in the back of our house. I lectured him about staying out of trouble; getting into a good college. I wondered how much longer my word would have any clout as he headed for the sullen shoals of teenage angst and rebellion. After all, while he loved me, how much could he reveal to his mom, especially the older he got and society pressured him to "act like a man." Already, my son had built up his defenses and set emotional boundaries.

Daniel had an explosive temper. He hit a girl when she taunted him for not having a dad. Once a week we trekked to the dreary office of the school's handpicked psychologist.

Some days I felt like our family portrait of mother, father and two sons had been defaced, as though someone had come along with a knife and sliced the father out of the picture. We were incomplete; or so I had been taught to believe.

Yet there were times when it all seemed to work. The boys had friends. Daniel was catcher for his Little League team. Alex had made honor roll again. We had a roof over our heads and money in the bank. Most of all, we loved each other.

But I had anger. While it fueled my ability to go to the newspaper and keep the house running, it depleted my energy, keeping me from a calmer, more peaceful place. The devastation of my husband's death left me vulnerable, believing I could heal by indulging in sensual pleasures.

So I bought lingerie from Victoria's Secret to please Ross, little panties that flattened the tummy and more. Aqua silk and leopard print bras that made me think I could keep him through sheer sexuality when all along my intuition was telling me that this man would never be there for me. I listened to complaints about his custody payments and his ex-wife. I even pretended to like his music.

Chapter Thirty-Three

"So how are you?" Paul asked. He slouched into a barstool next to me. His yellow necktie was rakishly loosened over an expensively, tailored white shirt. I felt my pulse change. Paul had dark hair and eyes. I felt his treacherous intimacy, but wolves compel us to look, even men who are wolves.

It was Friday night after work. The *Inquirer* had a news bureau in West Chester. The county seat, West Chester attracted art galleries and antique stores, gelato and coffee shops. It also offered a decent sampling of bars.

I had come to Vincent's to meet a girlfriend, but she called and canceled. That's when Paul walked in and took a seat next to me.

I looked at Paul holding a tumbler of bourbon. Lights flickered above the bar. His face was cast in shadow.

I had never understood his rude outbursts at school board meetings where he was the lone Democrat on the board among a cabal of Republicans. I had to admit he made good copy. He instigated shouting matches with the board's conservative Christians. Never one to shun the limelight, Paul became one of my "sources."

After I finished interviewing him, Paul, a lawyer, would veer off into *his* life story. We were off the record and he went on about whatever was irritating him that day.

Once we talked about my being a widow. Paul told me he was twelve years old when his father died. His mother remarried within nine months. From what I gathered from Paul, she was financially well off and didn't really need to remarry at all.

"It was inappropriate how little time she waited. She never cared about anyone but herself," I remembered him saying.

Now he signaled the bartender for bourbon.

"Linda and I are divorced," he said. "I went to the office on a Saturday. I came home around lunch and saw the U-Haul. My wife was moving out of our house and taking the furniture and my daughter to her mother's house."

"Oh, Paul, I'm sorry."

But I wasn't feeling sorry. The encounter had just become more intoxicating. Paul was smart. I was attracted to him.

Paul peered into the bottom of his bourbon glass. He stirred the amber liquid with the plastic straw.

"You know, I used to work for a larger, more prestigious firm, but office politics got in the way."

Our knees were intimately pressed together. Denise said chemistry, like love, was a mystery. I remembered John's long eyelashes, the shape of his hands on the steering wheel. I couldn't get enough of his touch, his smell, his body moving into mine. How easy it was when you were with a man you felt attracted to, rather than someone like Mack, the overweight airline pilot who was angry at women. Or Phil, who had no plan other than to hang out in a trailer home in New Mexico.

Then there was Ross. Days would go by when we didn't talk. The trophy girl I had been as *The Philadelphia Inquirer* reporter had faded for him and the sexual excitement was abating for me.

Orange chili pepper-shaped lights and a blinking red plastic martini glass strung over the bar brought me back to the present. Paul pulled his barstool closer. He told me he met his ex-wife, Linda, when he was twenty-eight years old.

"Why did you marry her?" I asked.

"Well, she didn't have much to say for herself. She was a ditz," he laughed. "She had auburn hair. Wait I get it. She was short, too, like me. I was almost thirty and it was time."

"Ah, yes the rite of passage. I can see that," I said.

"Yeah," he agreed. "Now look where it's gotten me."

His secretary had unexpectedly quit the week before. His law firm was running in the red. Linda, at the age of forty-three, was dating her twenty-nine year old lab assistant.

"She's an idiot," he said.

I was thinking she was getting sex and he wasn't.

He was so close. I could smell him, the alcohol . . . the faintest whiff of male sweat.

"You know I find you very attractive," Paul said. "I'd watch you at school board meetings and I'd think to myself, there is the kind of woman I need; strong, intelligent and independent. I've watched you walking down the streets here in town and think the same thing. You seem so confident, like you know who you are. And you're doing a hell of a job raising your boys on your own."

This man was truly a contradiction. He was rude and arrogant and self-centered. But he had noticed me, how I carried myself. I had watched him, too. I could sense when he walked into the room at school board meetings. I would pretend to casually look up from my notebook. Sometimes, our eyes met. I blushed when I felt him staring at me.

If only Paul knew how scared I was; scared I would make a mistake raising my sons, scared of being alone.

"You put up a good act," John once said to me. "But I know you are not as tough and confident as you want people to think." John, of course, had been right. John knew me. Love is a long, close scrutiny.

Paul leaned over, closer to me. His leg moved into mine. Then he started kissing me, sensually near the corner of my mouth, his lips traveling along the side of my face and back to my mouth. He was rubbing my arm, my hand reached for his. I loved his touch. My skin felt hot as we sat there in the dimly-lit bar.

Paul was asking me if I liked to ride. He owned a horse, although he was thinking of selling it. The upkeep was becoming more than he could afford. Fox hunting was his passion. He was teaching his daughter to ride. Riding was a prerequisite for the wealthy, the horsy set.

The bells should have gone off then, the red flags that Paul was into money and social climbing. I was a reporter, a lowly person on the social totem pole, relatively speaking.

"I know horses," Paul whispered. "You are like a thoroughbred."

I hoped he meant it, but my reporter's brain kicked in, suspecting he was reeling me in for the kill. Still, what harm was there in kissing him? I was so lonely that a little pain didn't seem like too high a price.

Paul paid for our drinks. Most of the streets were deserted now. I shivered and grabbed his arm as a bitter February wind kicked up on High Street.

The *Inquirer* parking lot was a few streets away from Paul's rundown, little office. I had walked past it many times; the small brown and green sign Paul C. Larson, Esq., leaning up against the dirty window sill in the old brick row house next to a florist's.

His lonely little office spoke of desperation and a man hanging onto the coattails of a wealthy mother who had never shown him tenderness. There was poverty; then there was *poverty*.

We got in the front seat of my Pathfinder. I turned on the ignition and cranked up the heater.

"I like you," I said. "I like that you're a rebel. You say what you want at school board meetings and don't care what people think."

"So, you like me?" he repeated with a teasing grin. "I'm warning you. I can be a real bastard."

This I knew.

He started kissing me, again. "Let's go over to my office. I have a couch in there."

His invitation was hardly surprising. He was drunk. But it was his way: the outbursts, the snide comments he made at school board meetings, the shouting at those who disagreed with him. He was rude. I let him sit there and touch me.

I wondered if it had been another woman sitting at the bar instead of me, if he'd have picked her up. I had been so willing and attracted to him, it was almost embarrassing. His bait was juicy. I sucked it up like a needy sponge.

"You've had a lot to drink. Why don't I drive you home?" I said regaining the upper hand.

He insisted he was fine. I searched his face. In the dim light of the parking lot, all I could see was the shadow of his mouth and his dark-rimmed glasses.

"I feel sick," Paul announced. Suddenly, he opened the passenger side door, leaned his head out over the parking lot. Nothing happened. Paul's urge to vomit passed. But his desire did not.

"Sex would be nice," he said picking right up where he'd left off. He was leaning against me, his hand groping me. "It would feel so good, wouldn't it? Come on. Let's go back to my office." He leaned toward me again.

Like a passenger on the Titanic, I refused to accept that the ship was going down. I just wanted to believe we could set sail together, the lawyer and the reporter living a passionate and rewarding life.

"Will you call me tomorrow? It's Saturday. We could go out," I said touching his arm. "We could have a date . . . a real date."

"Call you tomorrow? Why would I call you tomorrow?" It was said with nasty nonchalance. I had heard him use the same tone with school board members he disrespected.

I felt the chill of his rejection. We had hit the iceberg. I pushed against him.

Paul opened the car door. The light came on. He looked at me one last time and then let himself out of my car, his black trench coat flopping around his knees, a sad little boy in a man's outfit.

My would-be prince staggered off into the darkness of another cold West Chester night. I moved the car out of park and started the drive home. The highway seemed to lead nowhere. Even the houses were dark.

Prince Charming isn't supposed to die, I thought. I was supposed to be happy now in my fairy kingdom, not here sorting through more duds. Never believe the fairy tale, just learn from it. I wasn't a princess in a tower and Paul McCartney – or Paul Larson - wasn't going to rescue me.

Chapter Thirty-Four

When I was a junior in high school, I brought home a 'D' in algebra. I hated math and didn't understand it. During class, my mind drifted to the novel I was writing. Set in the court of King Charles II of England, it had courtiers and ladies-in-waiting, a dashing soldier and an auburn-haired beauty.

I was happiest when I was typing away on my Smith Corona. School work was an annoying distraction from writing. My father didn't see it that way.

"You'll never get into anything but a community college with grades like these," Dad yelled.

Humiliated, I shouted, "I don't care!"

My father's hand came out in a flash and he slapped me across the face. I felt my cheek sting. I ran out of the room in tears.

My father, the person I trusted the most, had struck me. Why? I challenged him. After that, I avoided confrontation.

When Jackson lied and told me his affair with a man had been "experimentation" and meant nothing, I didn't argue even though his homosexuality was obvious. When Alan, my newspaper editor, drank so much scotch he passed out in front of me, I stayed silent.

When men insolently called me a "feminist" because I had said something they found incorrigible, I let it go.

Then John came along. Passive, compliant women bored him. With John, I found my voice and my confidence. I could express myself and not lose him. With him, being rebellious meant standing out from the crowd. It made him desire me.

I needed to hold those lessons close, now more than ever. I needed to rest, to stop wildly running down blind alleys.

That night, I called my friend, Marcia.

"How's Matthew?" I asked.

"He has to get his basement cleaned out before he can put the house up for sale."

"Has he told his wife he wants a divorce?"

"Two months. If he hasn't told her by then, I'm through."

"So what about you?" she asked. "How are things with Ross?"

"Days go by and he doesn't call. And then there was this guy, Paul, the other night. He was so rude and drunk."

"I'm sorry," she said.

"Me, too."

I hung up with my friend. So many women trapped without a fresh eye to see what was happening. Not taking the time to stop, think and listen to their inner voices, their intuition. Not pruning and trimming the deadwood. I knew. I had become one of them.

A couple days later Alex came home after a visit with Gaby, Ross's daughter. They had walked in on Ross.

"He was making out with some woman on the couch. You'd think he'd come up with some new moves, but it was the same old thing," Alex said. She was young, probably in her thirties. Some woman he'd met at church.

Chapter Thirty-Five

I walked across the road to his neighborhood. I opened the heavy front door with brass knocker, calling his name.

It was dark inside except for one meager light in the family room, another money-saving gesture on his part, no doubt. He stepped out of the shadows. His broad shoulders looked even broader under the white tee shirt with the word "Head" on the front.

Ross viewed me impassively, made no attempt to touch me.

"So? Who is the new lady?" I asked.

"She's a friend, Susan." His tone was icy.

"I thought you loved me." The house was quiet, and my words landed like stones on a hard surface.

"I don't think we are a fit."

So this was it then. He was dumping me.

I thought of another life. We cooked together, listened to Sinatra. Afterwards, I curled up against him to watch a movie.

How had I fallen so far from the mark?

"You know, it must be wonderful to be you," I said. "There you are, the perfect dad, the perfect husband, whose horrible wife left you for no good reason that you can figure out, seeing as how you were the self-sacrificing breadwinner and she the blood-sucking bitch. Everyone is an object of your contempt. You have no heart, no empathy."

It was as if I had flipped a switch. Ross grabbed my arm, propelled me out into the foyer. Bob Dylan stared at us as he hung in a frame on the wall.

"Get out. Get out of my house," he shouted.

He stepped forward, his face contorted.

Pain shot through my arm as he squeezed it. He grabbed the door - opened it with one hand. The other hand pushed me forward without letting go. I was halfway out when I turned awkwardly to look back at him. If I hadn't moved fast enough, he would have crushed my shoulder as he slammed the door in my face.

I ran home, silently cursing him and my own stupidity. Alex warned me.

My heart pounding, I opened the sliding glass door and stepped onto my deck. "Are you out there? Can you hear me?" I whispered.

The forsythia bushes rustled in the breeze.

Almost three years had passed since John's death; three years while I searched for a haven and the security of a man. All I had really done was look for John.

John was irreplaceable. I finally understood that. Now I had to take Susan in my arms, love her and tend to her.

I remembered when Dad held me above the roaring surf.

"Here comes another hair comber, Daddy!" I squealed.

Again in a Heartbeat

I was five years old and had wisps of fine blond hair. My rose-colored satin bathing suit had strings that tied behind my neck, a glamorous little number chosen by my mother.

"Mommy! Watch!" I shouted.

Mother's brown hair blew in the sea breeze as she sat on the beach. A pale yellow sweater covered her thin arms. She watched us behind turquoise and rhinestone-studded sunglasses. She waved, just as the next white curl of ocean broke over Dad and me. When I looked up again, Mother had pushed her hair under a white rubber bathing cap and ventured to the shoreline. Tentatively dipping one toe into the icy water, she stood frozen, afraid to take the plunge.

I knew then I wasn't going to be like her. I wasn't going to be afraid and anxious. I wanted to experience it all, to feel the surge and excitement of the next wave. I believed in magic, that life was full of possibilities. I hadn't been wrong. I traveled to Europe. I became a reporter. John walked into my life. I had two healthy and attractive sons.

Like John said, nothing is the way it's portrayed in Hollywood. There hadn't been a happy ending. It is what it is. But there might be a new Once upon a time as I moved forward.

I stepped back inside the house and locked the sliding glass door. There was no explanation why John had to die. I remembered a Mary Oliver poem. Contentment comes when we stop asking *why* and flow with the current in the river of life. Without the flow, the river dies.

It was time to let the river carry me. Who knew where it would lead? I knew one thing. Not even death could stop me from dreaming. I was still a romantic.

Chapter Thirty-Six

Denise and I sat at a table sipping frosty mugs of beer. We looked out toward the turquoise ocean. Multi-colored beach umbrellas leaned at tipsy angles in the white sand. Teenagers played Frisbee and couples walked hand-in-hand along the shoreline shimmering in the August heat.

Denise lived on Long Beach Island, New Jersey. Long before my best friend moved here, I had been initiated into the pleasures of the island.

The summer after my sophomore year in college, I waitressed at an Italian restaurant on the bay. At night my girlfriends, who had landed jobs at Rite Aid and the Five and Dime, sat with me on the veranda of the Victorian house in Beach Haven where we rented rooms. We tasted the cool salty sea breezes and inhaled the lingering coconut scent of suntan lotion that clung to our clothes and our bodies.

"Light My Fire" blared from the stereo in the house across the street, where guys who were lifeguards by day and bartenders at night lived. They provided us with endless fascination and fodder for conversation as we sat in wicker rocking chairs on the veranda, smoking cigarettes and drinking beer.

We were young and the world lay at our feet.

Now as Denise and I talked, it was much the same, only we were older and, thankfully, wiser. There had been disappointments and heartaches, but one thing was constant. We had been friends going on four decades.

As the sun began to set over the Atlantic, we talked about her nasty new editor, her two divorces, Internet dating, the stories we were covering and the amount of work it took to put together a news article.

We talked about John and the day she introduced him to me under white dogwood trees above the parade field at Valley Forge Military Academy.

When I was in college, I roomed for a short time with a Dutch girl. Regina had left her home three thousand miles behind because a man she met one day offered her a plane ticket to Washington, D.C. if she would come and live with him. The United States was a dream come true for Regina who spent her entire life living on a houseboat in Amsterdam. When the relationship with the man took the inevitable downward turn, Regina and I found an apartment near the Smithsonian Zoo. It was Christmas when we moved in.

We plugged in a small ceramic green tree with cement-like gobs of "snow," cracked open a bottle of vodka and talked, weaving a tapestry of friendship until the early hours of the morning. We talked about all the idiot men we had known. We talked about what we wanted to do with our lives. Each of us believed the other would accomplish all she set out to do, when one day we would meet again and be famous. Men and women have relationships, Regina said, but women have friendships. They are sisters.

And Regina, who believed life was yours if you were willing to reach out and take it, was right. Friends offer acceptance and love, a harbor in the storm.

Epilogue

I picked up my pen and began writing in my journal.

What would I say to you if you could come back? What would I say about the years we have been apart? I would tell you how infuriating and wonderful our sons are. Alex got straight 'A's this year. He's quiet and keeps to himself. Still waters run deep. He misses you more than he can admit.

Every day Daniel looks more and more like you. Daniel is happy, I think because you spent so much time with him. He has a new puppy which he begged me for after Brandy died last spring. She's a black Lab. We named her Lucy. She's built like a small horse.

I would tell you about the forsythia bushes, how high they are . . . every spring they bloom radiant yellow like sunshine.

I would apologize for not being a better wife, kinder to you in your solitary battle with cancer. But you never wanted an apology. You knew long before I that the pain of losing you was almost more than I could bear.

Flirtation Walk, the trip to Yosemite, walking along the beach... it all seems like a dream. But it was real . . . enough to sustain me.

You would be proud of me. You knew I always wanted to write a book. I have started one. It's a love story.

Winter turned into the summer of 1998 and I took Alex and Daniel on a vacation to Arizona. We stood at the rim of the Grand Canyon and looked out toward eternity on earth.

In Arizona the prickly pear cactus grows low to the ground. It develops a hard skin almost an inch thick. Its spines cloak deceptively soft fuzzy patches. In early summer it produces an array of brilliant yellow and gold flowers. When the bloom fades, the edible fruits form.

One spring day a man stood under dogwood trees. He saw the thick skin, the flowers and the fruit. He felt the prick of the spines. He loved the beauty, despite the pain.

He loved me. And for that I would be there again in a heartbeat.

Made in the USA
Charleston, SC
19 September 2010